PATH TO THE
ENTREPRENATI ®

PATH TO THE
ENTREPRENATI®

~

Pace Klein

Path to the Entreprenati

Editor: Diane O'Connell
Cover Design: George Foster
Interior Design: David Moratto

LCCN: 2012931729

ISBN: 978-0-9851010-0-8

First Edition
Printed in the United Stated of America

To My Mom
&
Entreprenati Moms Everywhere

CONTENTS

THE REQUEST   1

Emerge and See   15

PART I   TAKE HOLD OF YOUR LIFE'S ADVENTURE

April Meeting   21

1   Riddle Me This   25

2   Begin at the Beginning   27

3   Webster in the Room   30

4   M.I.A.   33

5   See Where You're Coming From   36

6   No Vacancy   39

7   That's Nowhere to be Found   43

PART II   BECOME THE PERSON CAPABLE
OF ACHIEVING YOUR DREAMS

May Meeting   51

8   Ghost in the Machine   57

9   You're Sick   59

10   Me Happening to Me   63

11   Dem Bones, Dem Bones   66

The Tin   69
    12 Friends in Low Places   71
    13 Are You Chris   74
    14 Cut to the Chase   77
    15 Screwed by Evolution   80

PART III   DANCE THE DANCE

June Meeting   85
    16 Look Mom, No Hands   89
    17 Unboulder Your Shoulder   92
    18 Killing Time   96
    19 Bringing a Knife to a Gun Fight   99
    20 Stay Tuned   102
Charisse   105
    21 Join the Club   109
    22 Life in the Fast Lane   113
    23 Do I know You   116
    24 Eye of the Tiger   119

PART IV   EMBRACE & BE EMBRACED

July Meeting   125
    25 Dream a Little Dream for Me   129
    26 Come Hither   132
    27 The High Performance Memberless Organization 135
    28 Clowns to the Left of Me, Jokers to the Right 138
    29 Cornucopia   141
    30 In the Company of Yourself   143
    31 Handle with Care   147

32 Believe You Me   151
33 When Push Comes to Shove   154

PART V   LOOK AT THINGS DIFFERENTLY

August Meeting   161
34 What's Your Problem   165
35 In or Out   168
36 Wheel of Fortune   171
37 Present & Accounted For   174
Grain of Sand   177
38 Imagine That   181
39 Out of the Box and into the Fire   184
40 Chain Reaction   187
41 Lunar Navigation   189
42 The Usual Suspects   191

PART VI   GET IT TOGETHER

September Meeting   199
43 Frankly my Dear, I Do Give a Damn   203
44 I'll Just Let Myself In, Thank You   206
45 It's Not an Option   208
46 I Was Found, But Now I'm Lost   211
47 All Hands on Deck   213
The Letter   217

Author's Note   221

THE REQUEST

The mist spraying from the nostrils of the iron horse sculptures seemed so much like the breath of real horses in the cold of winter. But it wasn't winter and they weren't real. Breathing, but not really breathing, not really living. Made me wonder when was the last time I was really living ... maybe ten years ago, before dreams gave way to dreaming ...

I snapped out of my thoughts when I felt Glith's presence. Standing right next to my chair and looking like he'd always been there, despite his sudden appearance, he smiled when I turned my head his way. "Jesse, you're here!" he said. Startled, I quickly stood up to greet him.

We were meeting at a café near his home in *Place des Terreaux* on the *Presqu'île*, the peninsula between the Saône and Rhône rivers in Lyon. I'd taken the TGV train down from Paris and sat in the café, looking out at *La Fontaine de Bartholdi* on that March evening when Glith arrived at my table.

Dapper as always, he sported a perfectly fitted dark brown suit, beige open-collared shirt, five o'clock shadow, and wide, easy grin, as if just back from an afterparty of a *Vogue* fashion shoot. Yet I couldn't help but notice his clothes were uncharacteristically wrinkled, and his long hair, usually in a ponytail, flowed down to his shoulders. Curious, and I wondered why he'd called me down to Lyon for a special meeting. We typically met whenever he happened to be up in Paris on business about once a month.

He firmly shook my hand, placed his worn, though obviously expensive attaché case under the table, unbuttoned his jacket and sat down.

"She represents France," said Glith, pointing out at the statue of the horse-drawn chariot. "The horses represent the four great rivers of France, harnessed, yet untamed."

"Whatever," I quipped. "The Statue of Liberty has way more meaning."

Glith nodded. I guess even he couldn't argue with the big, green lady.

"But, you know, Glith, Bartholdi did a lot of cool sculptures ... you've seen the bronze lion he did for Paris, right?"

"Yes."

"Well, that's actually a smaller version of a giant lion he did for the city of Belfort. He made that one out of red sandstone ... from smaller blocks he pieced together ... and you can see how the different material, you know, sandstone versus bronze, affected the details."

"I didn't know the Paris lion had a big brother in Belfort."

"Three times bigger. Bartholdi made the Paris lion exactly one-third scale, which is interesting because ... whoa, let's hold it right there. You didn't call me down here to talk about this stuff. I can chew your ear off about it some other time."

"True, but finish your thought first."

I finished my thought and wound up rambling on some more about the sculptures, until Glith asked about the meanings behind the lions, but I didn't know.

Then, after some small talk to catch up since we last met, Glith propped his elbows on the table, leaned forward, and began speaking in a hushed tone.

"Jesse," he said, sharply narrowing his fierce blue eyes. "Now I'm going to tell you something you must promise to keep strictly between us. Will you promise me that?"

This caught me by surprise and without even thinking about it I heard myself say, "Yes, of course."

"It's something no outsider has ever known," he said. Then he paused, gathering his thoughts, or maybe his resolve. "Have you ever heard of the Knights Templar?"

The Knights Templar? What the heck is he talking about? I cleared my throat. "You mean, um, the knights who fought in the Crusades?"

"Yes, that's how people think of them. They were, in fact, created by the Roman Catholic Church to protect pilgrims traveling to the Holy Land."

"Okaaay ..."

"Hang in there, Jesse, I'll explain." He leaned back in his chair, took out a cigarette, lit up, and inhaled deeply. "In 1139, Pope Innocent II issued a decree, called the *Omne Datum Optimim* — Latin for 'Every Perfect Gift' — exempting the Templars from all national and local laws. This meant they could function within countries and across borders free from the rule of any king."

Glith stopped talking and motioned for the waiter. When he came over, Glith ordered an espresso. He then began thumbing his napkin, as he smoked and stared off into space. I could smell the sweet, fruity scent of his cigarette, little black cigar actually. He once told me he had them custom made in some place in Indonesia. Jakarta, I think. He finished the last drag, and stubbed it out in the ashtray.

"You see," he said, suddenly focusing his attention back on me with a jarring intensity, "the purpose of the decree was to facilitate the Templars' protective role, but there were those among them who saw within this miraculous freedom the seeds of a far more profound opportunity." Glith paused. His fiery focus drilled into me. "Can you imagine what this meant, Jesse, this unprecedented freedom?"

"Um, they were the first to turn right on red?"

Glith didn't laugh. "Open your eyes Jesse," he said, gesturing around with his hands, "see the possibilities ... see what they saw ... liberated from the constraints of the monarchs, they saw the opportunity to think and operate in entirely new ways ... to reimagine the very foundations of man's attitudes and approaches towards his worldly pursuits."

"Oh, is that all?"

"This is no joking matter; I'm about to tell you some-thing no outsider has ever known."

"Outsider to what? I don't understand?"

"Of course you don't. We're dealing with something that's remained hidden for seven centuries. You, at the moment, are an outsider."

Glith noticed the waiter approaching and sat back. He remained quiet as the waiter made his way to our table.

After the espresso was served, Glith carefully scooped out precisely a quarter spoonful of sugar and spread it as a thin layer across the top of his drink. "A properly made espresso will hold the sugar on top for a time," he said, as he waited for the fine crystals to slowly sink below the surface. He smiled up at the waiter, who bowed slightly and walked away. It seemed to be some sort of ritual they had, like sniffing a wine cork or something.

Apparently satisfied with the sugar's rate of descent, he stirred his drink and took a sip. He then put down his cup, raked his fingers through his thick, dark hair and said, "I'll explain a bit more ... and then I'm going to ask something of you. I've chosen you because I've come to trust you like no other outsider."

So, I was "chosen?" And I still didn't know what he meant by "outsider." I started to think he might not be dealing from a full deck. But that didn't square with what I knew about him. A highly driven, self-made man, he'd always been such a solid guy. Plus, he was so kind and generous to me and my mom after my dad died when I was a kid, and I'd been learning so much from him since being transferred to my company's Paris office four months ago. But now, with this bizarre scene unfolding, it struck me that I actually didn't know him all that well and he was a strange person.

"Look, I'm glad I've earned your trust, but I don't know if I'm ready for this stuff you want to tell me."

Glith grinned at this. "Let me continue, and then you can decide if you're ready or not — once you've heard a touch more."

I shrugged. "Okay, sure."

Nodding, he picked up the tale again. "Using their newfound freedom, this group of visionaries began by ushering in the world's first international branch banking system. Journeying noblemen could deposit money with the Templars at one location and make withdrawals at Templar stations along their routes, in their home countries or in distant lands. This was revolutionary."

Glith stopped talking as a couple passed by our table.

"The Templars then expanded their reach into many other areas of commerce," he continued. "Their businesses spanned the globe. They became nothing less than the first ever multinational corporation."

"Okay, but this all sounds like public information. What does it have to do with your secret?"

"The Templars amassed so much wealth, power and influence they eventually threatened the authority of the ruling class. In 1307, King Philip IV ordered the arrest of the Templars in France and Pope Clement V issued a decree instructing all monarchs to arrest the Templars and seize their assets wherever they could be found."

"Arrested for what?"

"Heresy, but it was a bogus charge."

"What makes you say that?"

"The Pope himself said it. He signed a declaration in 1308, called the *Parchment of Chion*, discovered in the Vatican secret archives centuries later, absolving the Templars."

"So what happened to them?"

"They were imprisoned, some even burned at the stake."

"And that was the end of them?"

"So people thought."

Glith must've known he'd hooked me because he said, "Jesse, I've told you all I can without your absolute commitment to keep this under wraps. What do you say; can you hear the rest?"

Apparently I'd been holding my breath. I exhaled. "Go on."

Glith winked. "The Templars weren't completely wiped out. Some of them survived. One small group in particular ... the clutch of enlightened entrepreneurs among them who had for nearly two centuries quietly lead their empire from behind the scenes escaped to form their own secret order. They became ..."

Glith broke off mid-sentence. He looked out into space. After a while, he turned his attention back to me. He leaned in and motioned for me to come closer. I leaned in so close our faces nearly touched and I could smell the cigarettes and coffee on his breath.

"They became," he whispered, *the Entreprenati*." He then sat back in his chair, and exhaled, as if relieved. "There, I said it ... I am Entreprenati."

I shook my head, bewildered. "I ... don't get it. I mean, Entrepre-what?"

Glith glanced around to assure himself no one else was paying attention. Then he responded in a low voice. "I know this must sound strange to you. Maybe even crazy. But I have confidence, Jesse, that it'll begin to make sense before long." His eyes searched mine and apparently saw enough to reassure himself I wasn't too far gone. "I am Entreprenati," he repeated. At my blank look he asked, "Have you heard of the Illuminati?"

I shrugged. "You mean the group conspiracy theorists think runs the world or something?"

"Close enough," said Glith, with a slight laugh.

I looked at him questioningly. "The Illuminati," he continued, "are reputed to possess arcane knowledge for masterminding the course of human events. The name means the illuminated ones."

"So they exist?"

"I'm not saying they do ... or they don't."

"What are you saying?"

"I'm saying the Entreprenati are the Illuminati of entrepreneurs. Enlightened entrepreneurs."

"Sooo ... you're enlightened businessmen?"

"Sort of. Not really." Glith paused for a moment, as he tapped his finger on his lower lip. "Whether or not one realizes it, Jesse, the animal spirits of entrepreneurism are at play in everything people do—whether one strives to succeed in a business or a job, at being a parent, spouse, or friend, or anything else. We're talking about enlightened *life* entrepreneurs."

What? Really? Sounded like a bunch of foolishness to me. But Glith was nobody's fool. So I couldn't make it all add up.

"Nothing about this Order has ever been known to the public," he continued, "not even its name or very existence. The Order has remained completely sub rosa for over seven hundred years."

"But why are you telling me this?" I asked, figuring it best to play the thing out and try to make sense of it all later.

"I've come to believe that some of the Order's guiding principles should be revealed to the public."

"But why?"

Glith peered at me intensely. After a while, his manner eased, a small smile crept across his face, and he began to speak again. "To be Entreprenati is to accomplish great things. Yet at the core of what it means to be Entreprenati lies a simple thing. A simple thing, but an all powerful one."

Glith reached his arm across the table and put his hand on my shoulder ... "it's the willingness and the ability to take complete responsibility for your own life," he said. "That's the foundation of it, the base upon which everything Entreprenati is built."

I frowned. *That's it?* "So you want to tell people to take responsibility for their lives?"

"No!" He shook his head and sat back. "Man, I never want to tell anyone how to live their life. I want to empower them to decide for themselves."

This didn't seem like any big secret to me. "Can't they do that now?"

"They could, if they knew they had this choice, *and* ... if they had the personal power to exercise it. Most people don't though. I'm talking about the choice to seek full expression of your authentic self."

"Um ... so you want to tell them they should ... ?"

Glith sighed and I watched his eyes dart from left to right as if searching through some book he'd read long ago. "How do I explain this?" he mused. Then he seemed to settle on a course and said, "I don't want to *tell* anyone anything, Jesse. Choice is at the heart of everything I'll be revealing to you. It's about *awakening* people to a choice they may not have been aware of, and their true ability to make this choice."

"Okaaay ... and then what?"

"Well, that'll be up to them. Most will do nothing. It's easiest. They'll squander the opportunity and remain blind to the choice. Of those who do seize the opportunity and bring the choice into their view, most will fail to rise to its challenge—they'll remain enslaved to themselves."

I shook my head. "If that's the case, why even bother?"

Glith smiled. "Because others, a few, might awaken and decide never to sleep again."

This was beginning to sound interesting—interesting, but still very strange. Was this Entreprenati thing for real? Was he actually going to reveal their secrets? I didn't know what to make of it.

"If we continue to keep the Entreprenati principles hidden," Glith went on, "even though many are hidden in plain sight, people won't have the chance to choose." He paused, then added firmly, "I now believe that everyone deserves their chance."

"All of a sudden? You just decided this now, after hundreds of years of secrecy?"

"Things have changed," he said, with a twinge of emotion I couldn't quite grasp. He then sat there, staring off into space, and repeated, "Things have changed ..."

After digesting this for a moment, I asked, "What things?"

Glith straightened and his features became firm. "I won't say right now. Maybe later, after you've spent a little time with these ideas." He opened his attaché case, took out a manila envelope and put it on the table.

I reached for the envelope, but Glith kept his hand on it. "If you take this, you'll be committing yourself to something that may have a profound effect on your life. Are you prepared for this?"

Good question. Did I even believe what he was saying? Could whatever was in there be that big a deal?

"I'm glad to see you're thinking about it," he said, as he studied my reaction. "It's not a step to be taken lightly."

I met Glith's gaze. "How can I commit to something when I don't know what it is?" I asked, almost belligerently.

For what seemed like forever, Glith's eyes locked onto mine and wouldn't let go.

Eventually, he said, "I'll tell you what I propose." He removed a stack of pages from the envelope and placed a few of them back inside. "Read just this, the introduction, and we'll meet again. You can let me know then if you want to read the rest of my manuscript."

"Manuscript?"

"Yes, I'm writing a manuscript designed to reveal some of the Order's guiding principles."

I scratched my head and asked, "If this is such deep stuff, what makes you think I'll be able to understand it?"

"Ah, now you're getting to the point of our meeting. I'm writing these principles in ways I believe could be meaningful to non-Entreprenati who might be open to such teachings. Although our wisdom is ancient, my manuscript will express it in a modern colloquial tone, in language today's seekers can hopefully grasp. I'll ask you to read it, and discuss it with me, so I can see if it's accessible to non-Entreprenati."

Weird, I thought. But I knew Glith to be a serious, accomplished man. And I never knew him to be anything but honest and well meaning. Plus, I owed him—not only because he helped me and my mom while I was growing up, but also because he'd taken such a strong interest in my life since I'd come to France.

"Okay, I'll do it."

"Good, but remember, this must be kept strictly between us for now."

"Sure, but if you're going to publish this stuff, why all the secrecy about it?"

"In time, my friend, in time." Glith grinned, "You understand," he said with a wink.

I didn't understand—not that or anything else really, but I decided to go along with it. I had nothing but the highest respect and deepest gratitude for the man, and would trust him, wherever it might lead.

Walking to the station later that night, I found myself moving quicker than usual, eager to get to the train so I could discover the contents of Glith's envelope. But when I finally got there, I didn't open the envelope. Something stopped me. Was it fear? A sense of unworthiness? What? All I knew for sure was that I wanted to open it, but couldn't. I wrestled with these conflicting emotions all the way home.

When I finally got to my apartment, I was exhausted. I could do little more than pull off my clothes and fall into bed. As I dozed off, thoughts flitted through my mind— just what would I find when I reached into the envelope in the morning?

—

The next morning, there it was. On the table, daring me. I brewed a pot of strong coffee, took a deep breath, opened the envelope and began to read Glith's introduction ...

Emerge and See

I am a member of the Entreprenati, an ancient secret order of misfits foolhardy enough to believe we could declare our own personal sovereignty, assume dominion over our own personal kingdoms.

The Entreprenati are the Illuminati of entrepreneurs—not just business entrepreneurs, but *life* entrepreneurs.

Here, the word "entrepreneur" is used in a far broader sense than its ordinary meaning. Every pursuit—in business or otherwise—is shaped by entrepreneurial forces, the raw ingredients of Entreprenati magic. This is true whether you work in a large company or a small concern. Whether your collar is white or blue. Whether you strive to be successful in your career, avocation, family life, or anything else that's captured your imagination or passion. There are Entreprenati in every realm.

> *The mark of the Entreprenati, whatever their endeavor, is belief in their ability to forge their own path through the thicket of human experience to bring themselves to their own success.*

Not to "arrive" at success, as if carried there in a chariot driven by others, but to bring yourself there, under your own power, in your own way, in your own time. Not success as others define it, but your own success, as you yourself define it.

People the world over yearn for success. But in whatever way they measure their own success, most feel they're not attaining it.

The story's the same in every enterprise, personal or professional. Many dive in, some drown, the bulk just tread water, others taste success to one degree or another, but only the tiniest sliver ever ascend to the rarefied ranks of the Entreprenati.

Why is this? Well, it's because most folks can't find their way out of a paper bag—their own personal paper bag that is.

A person's ultimate fulfillment exists in seeking full expression of his or her own individual spirit as a unique human being. Yet most people live inside a paper bag that has been cleverly constructed by their weaknesses to block them from even seeing this possibility, much less seizing it.

People are self-programmed to shun life outside the bag. Out there lies a ruinous wasteland littered with the squalid remains of the wretched unfortunates cruelly yanked from their bags by the callous hand of fate, along with the miscreants who couldn't or wouldn't construct their bag, or couldn't or wouldn't stay inside it. This repressive subliminal message, authored by our weaknesses and reinforced by our complicit brethren of the bag, becomes the story we tell ourselves, our false reality.

The Entreprenati reject the tyranny of the bag. Paper or plastic, we say none for us, thank you. We go *au naturel*. We've discovered that life beyond the bag, terrifying as it might appear to the uninitiated, can be a paradise for enlightened life entrepreneurs.

I won't tell you how to achieve this transcendental state because, quite simply, I can't tell you, as each person who ascends to the Entreprenati must do so through his or her own path.

Membership can't be given — it must be taken.

What I can do is reveal some of the guiding principles, some wisdom of the ages that may help you discover your own path to the Entreprenati.

Understand, however, that I use the words "reveal" and "discover" deliberately, as they're two distinct concepts. What's revealed is never the same as what's discovered. The form of the revelation plays a role in shaping the nature and quality of the discovery, as does the way the discoverer detects and processes it.

Imagine two hunters walking together in the woods. Further imagine that various game, though camouflaged to some extent, are potentially visible to both hunters as they go along. Yet one hunter may see more of the quarry than the other. And based on the way the animals are revealed — the distance, angle, movement, lighting, and intervening foliage — the less perceptive hunter may misidentify some of them, confusing them for other things. Moreover, he won't learn much if the other hunter simply points it all out to him. He'll experience true learning only if he discovers the game himself.

So, I'll do my best to reveal some of the Entreprenati principles in ways I hope will foster their most meaningful discovery by you — but the discovery part will be up to you.

Most fundamentally, this book invites you on an expedition. If you read this book, but fail to do so deliberately, fail to challenge yourself at every turn, and, most important, fail to mobilize yourself toward real change, real growth, then you'll be declining the invitation. You won't be joining us on the expedition.

That's fine if you find it amusing to fantasize you're on-board. But if you really want to come along, then throw your mind wide open and plunge into the text with the seriousness your life deserves.

I wish you an arousing journey. May you discover your own path to the Entreprenati.

PART I

TAKE HOLD OF YOUR LIFE'S ADVENTURE

April Meeting

Glith and I next met up on *Rue Juiverie*, a back street tucked into a quiet corner of *Vieux Lyon*, the old section of the city. I walked along the moonlit cobblestones to our rendezvous point, alone at that time of night, except, of course, for the gargoyles perched atop the medieval buildings lining the street on both sides, the air still damp from the day's April showers.

Glith appeared from a *traboule*, one of the many hidden passageways that snake throughout the maze of inner courtyards and winding streets of Lyon.

"A beautiful evening ... the moon, she hangs low tonight," he said, gazing up at the sky.

"Yeah, I guess she does."

"The first seven chapters of my manuscript," he said, handing me an envelope. He must've assumed I wanted to continue reading his stuff. He assumed right.

As I put the envelope in my bag, I began to realize he actually *did* plan to write a book. I'd half expected him to tell me it was all some kind of a gag, or test, or anything else that made some sense. But no, this was his story and he was sticking to it.

"Now come this way, Jesse," he said, motioning for me to follow him back into the *traboule*.

"I want to take you to a nice afterhours place. I think you'll like it."

"The introduction," I said, as we walked, "It seemed to be throwing down a gauntlet, challenging the reader."

"Yes, the book is designed to inspire you to take up a challenge, but not so much to challenge you, as to help you challenge yourself."

"Oh, so you want readers to challenge themselves."

"It's not about what I want—readers should want to challenge themselves. They should want to use this book as a catalyst to confront their own thoughts, their own feelings, their own behaviors ... to change themselves, to grow themselves."

I nodded as if I understood, but so much about this whole Entreprenati thing I just didn't understand. What did it all mean? I figured I'd continue to follow his lead and see where it took us.

When we arrived at the afterhours place, Glith exchanged gestures with a burly man at a thick iron door, and he let us inside. As we passed into the warm, humid bar, it felt strange to be the one *not* left outside.

We were ushered through the dimly lit, smoky main room to a small, private table off on the side, half hidden behind a green silk curtain. Glith ordered a Cognac, so I thought I'd try one too, seeing as I was in France and all.

A few minutes later, the waiter returned with two squat, pear shaped crystal goblets, with just a splash of drink barely covering the bottoms.

Rich musical rhythms filled the space as we sipped our Cognac. I'd never had it before, and it tasted like turpentine to me, but Glith seemed to savor his with delight, so I guessed it must be an acquired taste.

We were relaxing, taking in the colorful sights, sounds, aromas, and vibes of the place, when Glith reached into his jacket pocket.

"I found this old picture of me and your father when we were about your age, just a few years after college," Glith said, handing it to me.

"Fishing, of course," I said with a big smile.

"Yes, your father definitely loved to fish."

As I studied the image, my thoughts drifted back to our summer trips to the coast ... digging my fingers into the black, moist earth in pursuit of nightcrawlers wriggling back into their holes under the glare of my flashlight ... the plump, juicy ones that made the best bait ... the next day, off to the jetty with our tackle box and poles. A jetty, not a dock, wharf, port, or quay, as my dad would explain to me each year in great detail, so I'd know the differences. I didn't really care, but listened carefully because he sure did.

"What he really loved was the ocean," I said, remembering how I'd often felt alone on the jetty, my dad sitting next to me, but not really there, his mind lost somewhere out at sea.

"That he did matey. But he must've loved public relations more because he chose that over his blue mistress, right?"

"Maybe, but I doubt it."

"Why do you say that?"

"Well, he almost never talked about his job. He talked a lot about his blue mistress as you put it. And when he did talk about his job, he never seemed excited about it. I was only twelve when he died, but even I could see that."

"Hmm ... that's strange. I wonder why he jilted his flame for the cold embrace of PR."

I started wondering the same thing myself. I never thought about it before. I guess he had to. He must've had no choice. Why else would he do it? But why would he have no choice?

"I don't know," I finally muttered under my breath, suddenly feeling bewildered. Glith took a drag on his cigarette, and blew the smoke out the side of his mouth, while looking at me and nodding his head as if I'd just answered his question. Then he turned away and didn't say anything more. I spent the rest of the night grappling with his answered question, which had become my unanswered question.

Glith later lead me out of the *traboule*, bade me a brisk farewell, and I headed down the block toward the station.

As soon as I got to my seat on the train back to Paris, I immediately opened the envelope, pulled out the first set of chapters of Glith's book, and began to read ...

1

Riddle Me This

If you're like most people, your life makes sense to you. But are you thrilled by your sensible existence? Probably not, but you're self-programmed to keep on keeping on.

Most people never seriously consider the possibility of life outside the comfortable confines of their personal paper bag. Sure, you may daydream about it, but only in a whimsical sense, as if lusting after forbidden fruit. Actually entering this expanse, rather than merely fantasizing about it, requires you to face your fears, to summon the kind of strength few possess. It also requires you to believe you can do it, that you can emerge, that you can survive, and indeed flourish on the outside.

But you're programmed to believe you must remain securely ensconced within. When faced with the prospect of an adventure that lies out there in the great unknown, you're programmed to panic. A panicked mind seeks only one thing—a safe refuge. The "danger" passes and your life returns to normal.

Though this programming is stout, you're not a computer.

You have a choice.

Are you self-aware enough and courageous enough to take a peek outside—to see for yourself how glorious an unshrouded life might be? Or will you be dominated by your programming and run back inside your paper bag with your tail between your legs?

A circus elephant can be tied to a post with a string and he'll stay there. He can walk away at any time, but won't, because he's been programmed to think he can't. When he was small and weak, the string constrained him. When he grew big and strong, his mind constrained him.

> *Escaping the paper bag is, first and foremost, a state*
> *of mind—an Entreprenati state of mind.*

Your view of the world creates your reality. If you view the world through a scarcity and fear mentality, this restricts your choices and you never see the true range of possibilities. If you think you lack the personal power to take hold of your destiny, vanquish your foes, overcome your obstacles, and steer your own ship, it'll be a self-fulfilling prophecy.

> *Why not manifest a brighter reality?*

Why not behold a world in which all things are possible, charge your vision with the power of its inevitability, and then go out and make it happen—even if others tell you it can't be done? Hey, I'm just asking.

2

Begin at the Beginning

~

Step back! barks Yoshi's drill sergeant. Yoshi, soaked in a cold sweat, stands at the edge of a rocky cliff, his heels teetering over the abyss, as he quivers head to toe. Scrambled thoughts and images careen and collide through his terror-struck mind. This will be his first time rappelling off a mountain—or not.

It's said that a journey of a thousand miles begins with a single step. But not all steps are created equal. Many people want to take their life in a new direction but can't make it out of the starting block. This first step does them in.

> *The promise of a journey of a thousand miles ends with a single nonstep.*

Fear is one reason. That's Yoshi's hangup. He's attached by a rope, yet it's still a petrifying prospect to step off a perfectly good mountain for the first time. Until you experience this first step, you can only imagine you'll fall to your death. Once you take the first step, however, you feel the sense of being suspended in air, held by the rope, and your fears are exposed as the charlatans they are. Similar encounters occur in our day-to-day lives, such as the first time you address a sizable audience or otherwise confront your fears. That first step is a snarling vicious beast blocking your way.

Pain is the other reason. Say you want to start an exercise program or learn a new language. But the thought of joining a gym and suffering through all the grueling work pains you, as does the dread of possibly embarrassing yourself. The same goes for the idea of enrolling in a language course and suffering through all that mentally exhausting work, plus the dread of possibly embarrassing yourself in that new arena. Of course, all the imagined pain is overblown. But it's real to you. It's the snarling vicious beast.

So, a beast blocks your path. What to do?

Heed the three rules of beast blockage of course.

Rule number one: When a beast blocks your way, acknowledge his presence. He's there; don't pretend the road's clear.

Rule number two: Marvel at the power of your imagination. That's a mighty fine beast your imagination has conjured up, complete with flesh-tearing claws, thick crooked fangs, piercing red eyes, rancid snot dripping from his flaring nostrils, and a stench so putrid it could make a skunk wince.

Rule number three: Slay the beast. He's just a figment of your imagination, so lop off his head with your imaginary sword. You do this by taking the first step. Step off that mountain. Step into that gym. Step into that language course.

Don't think in terms of "getting started" down the road. First things first—see the beast in all his imagined glory, then smite him in all his actual nonexistence. After that, after you've slain the beast by taking your first step, celebrate your victory. Then you can light out on your merry way.

The key is to recognize the first step as a separate stand-alone challenge that must be met and conquered in its own right. It's not simply the first step of many. It's a fundamentally different thing.

> A journey of a thousand steps is actually two journeys — a one-stepper, which is the beast, followed by 999 steps.

What beast is blocking your path? Acknowledge it. Marvel at it. Annihilate it.

3

Webster in the Room

~

2010 was a defining moment for Sharon. An eternity at the time, now but a moment in time. She lost her mother to cancer and she lost a marriage into which she had poured her heart and soul for six years, only to come up horribly empty.

There was always a part of Sharon that expected so much more out of life than ever seemed to be in the cards for her. Yet she stubbornly clung to her impossible dream. Even as her father descended into the depths of the bottle, as her family struggled to keep afloat, and as she later wrestled with the demons of her broken childhood, she always dreamed that one day she'd be somebody, that she'd matter in this world. But she wasn't so sure of this in 2010. The impossible dreamer within Sharon withered, and of all the losses she suffered that year, this was the most devastating.

Before her marriage fell apart, she dreamed of going back to school to become an architect. Working as an administrative assistant at a construction firm, she dreamed of one day designing buildings that would reach to the sky. But now, with nothing but a low-paying job and no support from her ex-husband, she realized this dream was dead, along with the rest of her dreams. She would never amount to anything. Never matter in this world. She resigned herself to her new fate.

We all face defining moments. And here's what's vital to understand about those pivotal junctures in our lives:

> *At each of our defining moments, either we define it or it defines us.*

It's really this simple. Unfortunately, simple realities are often the most elusive. Simple doesn't mean obvious, and it doesn't mean easy.

What's equally simple, though no more obvious or easy, is this—the choice is ours. While a defining moment may bring new forces to bear upon your life, you alone hold the power to determine how you will change in response to these forces. The wind blows in a new direction; will you accept whatever new course results, or will you reset your sail?

Sharon made her choice, even if by default. She allowed the moment to define her. That's a shame. She could have made a different choice.

There are two reasons why people allow themselves to be defined by their defining moments, rather than the other way around:

> *Either they fail to perceive the defining moment, or they underestimate the capacity of the human spirit.*

When a friend needs help but it would require sacrifice or hardship on your part to step in, for instance, you can always reason why you shouldn't get involved. It's none of your business. He probably doesn't want your help. It's his own fault. Someone else is the more appropriate source of help. He wouldn't do it for you. It's too risky, too much work, and so on. But in failing to step in, for whatever reason, you allow the moment to define you as someone who doesn't come to the aid of your friends. You failed to perceive what was actually at stake — a moment of opportunity to define who you are.

Here, however, Sharon couldn't avoid perceiving that a defining moment was upon her. It's hard not to notice when your life's being ravaged. But she underestimated the capacity of the human spirit — its capacity to achieve in the face of adversity, to persevere, to endure, to overcome, to triumph.

When we behold the stunning achievements of luminaries past and present, we are at once both admiring them and admiring ourselves — marveling at the greatness in them, as well as in us. Their achievements inspire because they signify what we humans are capable of. Unfortunately, such inspiration is all too fleeting for most people, rarely translating into lasting belief. Like most, Sharon didn't know she had it in her.

Notice we're not saying Sharon lacked the capacity to triumph over her adversity, but that she failed to know she had this capacity. It's a crucial distinction. The human spirit manifests itself in the realm of mind over matter. Consequently, we can summon only so much of its awesome power as we believe exists within us.

4

M.I.A.

As Shakespeare so aptly put it, life can be "a tale told by an idiot, full of sound and fury, signifying nothing." Are you that idiot? Is your life full of sound and fury, signifying nothing?

All too many people run around like whirling dervishes — phones ringing, devices buzzing, emailing, texting, meetings, faxes, webinars, power lunches, conference calls ... but, often, when it's all said and done, much is said, little done.

It's like an amusement park ride. You're out there moving and shaking, but when the ride's over you're deposited right back where you started.

I'm not saying this is you. That's you saying it.
Listen to yourself.

Oh, the joy of being busy. Everyone yearns to attain this blessed state. Let's face it, you're either busy or pretending to be busy. Better yet, you're "super busy." And then there's the pinnacle of busyness — "crazy busy." Ahh, nirvana.

But busy is as busy does.

You can do one thing well. You can do two things okay. You can do three things poorly. Machines can multitask.

Depending on their design, they can do any number of things perfectly, all at the same time. Humans, not so much.

Your mind doesn't care whether or not it's functioning most productively, whether or not it's functioning so as to best advance your life. That's your job. If you choose to have it think about more than one thing at a time, it'll do so — it just won't do it so well.

Now, being busy isn't necessarily the same as multitasking. You can do one thing at a time and jump from thing to thing. But the mind will switch gears only so fast. Get too busy and your mind will wind up thinking about different things at the same time, which is multitasking, which, once again, people don't do well.

Even if you're not multitasking, you still may be screwing up your mind's ability to operate effectively. Running around like a whirling dervish means your mind is constantly being interrupted, robbing you of focus. Now, maybe you can work effectively without a high degree of focus. There's a name for that kind of work — unimportant. Is this really what you think of your work? If not, why are you treating it like that?

Busy can be good, but it can also be bad. When is it a good thing and when is it too much of a good thing? The answer depends on you, what you're doing, and what you hope to achieve.

The point here is to get you thinking about your busyness. Disrobe it, cast a critical eye on it, see it for what it actually is. Is yours a powerful ally helping you accomplish your goals or a grotesque parasite eating you alive?

> *Most fundamentally, you should reject its unde-*
> *served status as an object of desire.*

The legitimate object of your desire should be to reach the truly meaningful goals you've set for yourself. Busyness is nothing more than a (potential) means to this end. To the extent it serves this purpose, bring it on. Otherwise, get busy getting less busy. Yes, you can do this. The sky will remain firmly in place.

Busyness is a false god. Stop praying at that bogus altar.

5

See Where You're Coming From

⌒

Grimy, grueling work plunged Ron into the life of the laborer, a battleground of hardship and struggle, and of dignity. He also got a front-row seat to society's raw underbelly, a savage caldron of suffering and misfortune where hapless hordes grind out their days in the night of their hopes and dreams. Growing up on the wrong side of the tracks produced a bounty of treasures in Ron's development.

Where did life start you out—what gifts did you reap in beginning your relationship with the world from that initial vantage point?

Many people were born poor, or a minority, or missing one or both parents, or whatever, and because of this, they believe they're disadvantaged. But they're wrong.

Looking at the world from the bottom up spawns insight that can't be gained from any other angle. This is a prize of inestimable value. It's a precious opportunity to take on the world with this unique take on the world—armed with first-hand knowledge of how society works on the ground level. That's an advantage those poor rich kids will never have.

Now, this isn't to say being born with a silver spoon in your mouth isn't also an advantage. It's just a different advantage, not a better one.

This goes for all your circumstances—ethnic, religious, geographic, aptitudinal, familial, and so on. Even folks afflicted with physical or mental disabilities have achieved all manner of greatness, such as Stephen Hawking, Ray Charles, and Franklin Roosevelt. No one's disadvantaged—we're all *diff*advantaged.

Some people are smarter than you in one way or another, more athletic, artistic, mechanically inclined, better looking, or you name it, but no one has your special mix of attributes, coupled with your particular background. These are your circumstances, yours alone. How you embrace them determines your perspective, which, in turn, determines your very being—everything you are, everything you can become.

> *Your perspective is the most vital aspect of your being.*

It filters, colors, and shapes your world. You don't see life so much through your eyes, as through your perspective.

There are seven billion sets of human eyes on the planet. Train them on the same spot and they'll all see the same thing. Yet the owners of those eyes will see different things.

> *Like an impressionist artist standing between you and the world, your perspective interprets what your eyes are telling you is out there, delivering your own personalized version of reality.*

Does your reality-rendering artist create your version of reality using brush strokes that are short and precise or broad and sweeping? Colors that are somber and subdued, or vibrant

and intense? Emphasizing individual aspects or overall com-
position? Focusing head-on or at one or more angles? Soften-
ing the edges or sharply delineating them? And what of
transience versus permanence? How does it depict the light
of life in its changing qualities? Does it accentuate immediacy
or the effects of the passage of time? The elements themselves
or the shadows and ever-shifting reflections they cast?

To understand yourself or anyone else, you must get in
touch with the reality-rendering artist within. The style of
each person's reality-rendering artist is influenced largely by
his or her circumstances, but it's ultimately determined by
how he or she embraces those circumstances. Can you cherish
your circumstances — the beautiful along with the ugly —
even as you strive to transcend them? The Entreprenati can.

6

No Vacancy

Wow, you are seriously pumped up. Congratulations, you must be about to do something important, something that'll make an impact in your life and the lives of others. Tell me, are you a marketing executive about to present a national campaign proposal to a major client? A comedian about to go out on stage before a large audience? A doctor about to perform potentially lifesaving surgery? Fantastic, that's a superb opportunity. Time to shine.

Wait, what's that you say? You're worried you might blow it? How pitiful.

> When the game's on, and you're energized by the desire to perform, that's awesome. But if you're stressed over the specter of nonperformance, that's lame.

Others may tell you it's only natural to fret over the risk of screwing up. Sure, and it's also natural to go nowhere in life. That's where most people go, so join the crowd, if that's your cup of tea. Otherwise, read on.

When it's time to perform, but you're not really into it, only a small part of your mind will be engaged in pulling the bare minimum number of levers just enough to carry you through the movements, while the rest of your mind will be wandering off doing its own thing—reminiscing, perhaps, about a song that mesmerized you in high school, or planning what you're going to eat for dinner, or whatever else strikes its fancy.

When you're at least somewhat into it, more of your mind will be pulling more of the levers to increase your performance, but much of your mind will still be floating around in the cosmos.

Now, when you have a passion for what you're doing, this passion will permeate deep into your mind, throughout the conscious and subconscious, fusing it all together into a concentrated unity of focus on the task at hand—to pull, not just some, but all the available levers, and to do so with the speed and precision necessary to drive the human machine to its full potential.

But, if visions of failure creep into your mind, whether into the conscious or subconscious, your mind's singular bearing can be shattered.

If the encroachment is limited to fleeting visions, no significant parts of the mind will be distracted from pulling their levers. It'll be like a stranger just passing through. You may, on some level, notice him in your periphery, but this won't impact what you're doing. The stranger, in turn, will sense he's not welcome and will move on from this inhospitable place.

If, however, you start to worry about the intruder, what damage he might cause, and how you might avoid his wrath, then you breathe life into him.

> *He'll sense the attention and consider it an invitation to settle into your mental living room.*

He'll put up his feet and demand more and more attention. As you feed his escalating need, his energy will build, his appetite will grow, and larger parts of your mind will be distracted from pulling their levers. The performance of your machine will fall precipitously, and the risk of screwing up will soar.

Eventually, if your mind pays enough attention to this gruesome guest, he'll take up residence, demanding to be treated like a member of the family. If the invasion reaches this level, your mental family will be living in horror of this insatiable fiend they've unwittingly allowed to infest their home.

At some point, significant parts of your mind will start pulling their levers in disharmony with the overall operation, inhibiting your ability to produce your best results, and, in the extreme, even a complete seizing up of the machine will become possible.

Ironically, this whole sorry mess resulted from your attempt to prevent it.

Imagine you're a racecar driver rounding a turn bordered by a concrete wall. That wall is the stranger. If you focus on where you want to go, merely noticing the wall in your periphery, you'll roar through the turn and onto the ensuing straight like a champion. But, if you start paying attention to the wall, it'll grow into a throbbing colossus, diverting your focus from the course ahead. At best, you'll be impeded from going through the turn at full speed. At worst, you'll crash right into this monster you've created.

When your mind entertains debilitating visions of calamity, it's because you're thinking in terms of "not." You're "not" going to hit the wall, "not" going to bomb on your presentation, "not" going to blow the surgery.

This is the sign of the stranger—"not."

You must allow the stranger to pass on through. The stranger must remain a stranger—a stranger in a foreign land. Your mind must be this foreign land—foreign to the "not" way of thinking.

So, rather than think you're "not" going to hit the wall—believe you "will" roar through the turn. Rather than think you're "not" going to bomb on your presentation—believe you "will" deliver it with mastery. Rather than think you're "not" going to blow the surgery—believe you "will" ace it.

Believe you will—take hold of your life's adventure now.

7

That's Nowhere to Be Found

After nine good years, Sean's restaurant suddenly finds itself in death's grip. The area's dominant employer moved out, taking away the bulk of his customers. Now his business is hemorrhaging cash, hanging on by a thread.

Sean faces a difficult decision.

His basic options are to close up shop, relocate, downsize, or try to sell the business.

The thought of shuttering what he worked so hard to build is painful. Relocating would require him to take out a loan to pay for the move, an investment he's loath to hazard. Downsizing would spell hardship for the laid-off staff who've become like a second family to him. Selling the business would mean getting a pittance for his life's work.

This is definitely a difficult decision.

So, what does he decide to do? He decides to cut prices and increase advertising in an effort to draw in new customers. Hmm ... I don't recall this being one of the options.

There's a reason why Sean or anyone else faces a difficult decision in the first place. It's because you're torn between different choices, each of which presents its own mix of pros and cons that's far from ideal.

But what's really vexing about the decision is this—your choice will determine what world you're going to live in. Each choice either leaves you mired in your current world or else it thrusts you into a different world.

> *In essence, life is knocking at your door, asking you*
> *to choose which world you want to live in.*

If Sean decides to give up the ghost, he'll be living in the world of the failed business owner. This world is filled with no small amount of darkness, but it does short-circuit the pain, and it also leads to the possibility of a new beginning. In this world, he'll be winding down operations, selling off equipment, cancelling vendor accounts, negotiating his way out of his contracts and other obligations, explaining his decision to employees, customers, friends, and family, and grappling with the emotions such a course arouses in a person. Depending on the situation and the individual, this world may be filled with guilt or pride, a sense of failure or of relief, regret or a new lease on life.

If Sean decides to move the restaurant, he'll be living in a different world—one filled with the excitement of the move, but also the high-stakes drama of doubling down, putting even more money at risk.

If he decides to downsize, he'll thrust himself into the world of the ship captain battling to save a vessel foundering in a storm—throwing the unnecessary overboard, battening the hatches, hoping to ride it out to a better day.

If he decides to sell the business, he'll enter the world of the manager who hands over the reigns of a losing team. This world involves living on the sidelines, watching someone else try to save what you lost.

In such a situation, it's natural to yearn for a better choice than any life has laid at your doorstep. Yearn as you might, however, it's time to make the tough call. To decide which of these worlds you're going to live in. You won't be living there forever, but you will for a while, and it could be a long while. Yet, Sean did what so many people do—

He chose to live in a world that doesn't actually exist.

The world in which he saves his business by cutting prices and spending more on advertising doesn't exist.

The lifeblood of a business is positive cashflow. When it reverses direction and gushes outward, rapidly draining the bank account, the last thing you should do is reduce margins and increase discretionary spending aimed at building a new customer base over the longer term (worse, a customer base of cheapskates). In fact, this will only hasten the demise.

To his credit, Sean didn't turtle. He swung into action and this is to be admired. When life punched him in the face, he punched back.

Nevertheless, the world in which Sean saves his business by cutting prices and spending more on advertising doesn't exist, but that's where he chose to live.

Three months later, broke and broken, Sean is forced to throw in the towel, laying off his staff and abandoning his space and equipment to his creditors.

Sean isn't alone in deciding to live in a nonexistent world—many people make this choice.

Now, if this were simply a matter of bad judgment, it wouldn't be very interesting. No, what we're dealing with here is something different. We're dealing with those whose minds are playing tricks on them.

We're not talking about overactive imaginations. In fact, we can't be — because they don't exist either. An overactive imagination is an oxymoron.

But Sean's choice isn't the product of an imaginative mind. It's the product of a mind in denial of the difficult choice it faces. Had he invented and implemented a potential new solution to a classic problem, we'd have applauded him as imaginative in thought and bold in action, whatever the outcome. What he did, however, was to choose a known non-solution. Life came knocking on his door, asking him to choose which world he wanted to live in. Not liking any of the worlds life had on offer, and unable to conjure up a new one, Sean chose to live in a world that doesn't exist. This was neither imaginative nor bold.

As tragic as this is for Sean, it's far worse for you.

If this problem were limited to dire situations at critical junctures in your life, then at least you could be on the lookout for it. Unfortunately, it's a problem of everyday life.

Every day, life is there, on your doorstep, knocking at your door. Every day, it's asking you which world you want to live in. Every day, you have a choice to make. Alas, if you're like most people, every day you choose to go Sean's way.

> *For most people, the world in which they fulfill their ambitions by living the kind of life they've chosen to live simply doesn't exist.*

That's the bad news. The good news is that life knocks on your door every day. So, every day you get the opportunity to answer the call anew. How will you answer it today?

PART II

BECOME THE PERSON CAPABLE OF ACHIEVING YOUR DREAMS

May Meeting

The ideas from Glith's manuscript were rolling around in my head as I strolled through *Parc de la Tête d'Or* on a balmy spring afternoon — my personal paper bag, circus elephants, beast blockage, worlds that don't exist, *diff*advantages, whirling dervishes, savage cauldrons, defining moments, false gods, reality-rendering artists, revelation versus discovery, that stranger who must be banished, and on and on. So many ideas from just the first few chapters, so many questions.

I eventually made my way to the zoo, where I cleared my mind by watching the Capuchin monkeys eat the fruits and vegetables laid out for them by the zookeepers.

"Judging from your smile, you must be enjoying the show," said a familiar voice from over my shoulder.

I turned my head to see Glith standing at my side, also taking in the scene.

"Yes," I responded. "It's fun to watch them ... but, you know, it's also kind of sad."

"How so?"

"Well, I don't know, it's just ... a few minutes ago, when they gathered by the back door, staring at it, waiting for their meal to come out ... it just seemed sad to me."

"Did they look sad?"

"No, no, they actually looked pretty peaceful ... but I guess I was thinking they'd be happier if they were out getting their own food, you know."

"Yes, I see what you're saying, but some species, like these monkeys, seem to find comfort in being provided with food at a set time and place every day, without having to fear their predators in the wild."

"Huh, I guess it's okay then."

"Okay for them maybe, but others, like those tigers over there ... rather than look back at the feeding door, they look to the outside, pacing the perimeter, seeking a way out."

"Fine for a tiger," I said with a chuckle, "He doesn't have to worry about being eaten himself."

"True, but there are other dangers, like starvation for one. A free tiger is under relentless pressure to locate and chase down prey."

"So you'd think they'd enjoy the easy life here, you know?"

"No, the tiger won't submit to being mastered by others. He needs to make his own choices, go his own way, thrill to the hunt, run wild and free, come what may."

We stood for a while longer watching the monkeys finish their lunch, but my mind was now more on the tigers.

"The next set of chapters," Glith said, handing me an envelope.

"The first were really interesting," I said, placing the envelope in my bag, "But I wondered why you didn't give specific instructions at the end of the chapters."

"Really? Why is that?"

"Well, your chapters led me more to questions than to answers. Even your questions led me to more questions."

Glith grinned and clapped me on the shoulder. "Jesse, that's the best compliment you could have given me."

As I looked puzzled, he continued, "Remember I told you my book will be designed to help readers challenge themselves?"

"Uh-huh."

"Well, different people need to challenge themselves in different ways — by asking themselves different questions. My book will respect these differences. It'll create a learning environment where readers can discover their own questions. This is the first step. The answers will come later ... but not for everyone."

"What do you mean?

"Many will ignore the questions or spend just a moment in brief thought ... only those who afford the questions serious reflection might find their answers."

Serious reflection? Brief thought? Hmm ... I wondered which camp I was in ...

After some time at the zoo, we drove off in Glith's car to spend the day in Beaujolais. Glith said he wanted to "roam the wine country."

Later in the afternoon, we stopped at a vineyard and sat at a table on the patio behind the farmhouse, over-looking the rows of grapes. As we sipped our wine and enjoyed the warm, fresh country air and vast fields laid out before us, Glith mentioned that my mom had once considered becoming a *sommelier.*

"What's that," I asked.

"A wine expert," he said, swirling his Chardonnay and holding it up to the sun.

That remark infuriated me. Why the hell would Glith speak of my mom in *that* context?

"I'd rather not talk about her, if you don't mind," I said, trying to contain my anger.

"Oh, but I do mind. She was a special lady and I see no reason why we shouldn't celebrate her memory."

I put my elbows on the table, dropped my head down onto my hands, and rubbed my temples. "So you think drinking herself to death made her special?" I barked, as I snapped my head up, unable to control my rage. "You think I should celebrate that I couldn't save her, that I felt relieved when she was gone, relieved that I could finally go on with *my* life? Is that your idea of a celebration?"

"But you couldn't go on, right? You haven't."

"No son should feel the way I did at his mother's death."

"True," said Glith, standing up. He came around to my side of the table, knelt on one knee next to me, and placed his hand on the nape of my neck. "She had no right to make you feel that way. No right to rob you of the sadness you should have felt."

I heard what he said, but couldn't process it. Tears filled my eyes and my vision became as blurry as my thoughts. Glith squeezed his grip tighter and said — "Can you forgive her?"

"Forgive *her*?"

"Yes, she made bad choices. You made fine ones — to sacrifice a part of your life, a part of yourself, starting at an early age, to help her, first with her depression, then with her drinking. Can you forgive her for her bad choices? And for their damaging effects on you?"

I couldn't answer his questions. My guts were all twisted up. Eventually, he released me from his clench, stood up, and walked away. As I wiped the tears from my face, I felt like something inside me had left along with Glith, something I was better off without.

Later, as we continued to tour the countryside in his car, we discussed the first set of chapters. I didn't understand everything he said, but I thought I got most of it, and it was starting to make more sense to me. He sure didn't seem crazy. Yet I could tell he was completely convinced the secret, ancient Entreprenati Order existed and he was a member of it. I still didn't know what to make of this.

That night, back at my apartment, I sank into my easy chair, opened the window to enjoy the soft Paris evening, reached into the envelop and began to discover what Glith had given me this time ...

8

Ghost in the Machine

～

The world doesn't move for small people.

To move the world (or even your patch of it), you must be able to effect meaningful change in the thoughts, feelings, and behaviors of others. To set minds, hearts, and bodies in motion. This takes a big you.

You're going to have to become a bigger person if you're ever going to achieve your dreams. Because, let's face it, you're not that person now.

Don't think your problem is a lack of opportunity. It's a lack of you. There's no shortage of opportunity. It's all around us. You're just not worthy of it. Not good enough. Not ready.

We're not talking about skills.

> *We're talking about you — the spirit, the soul, the essence of who you are.*

Yes, skills are needed, but you already knew that. People are forever talking about acquiring and sharpening skills. You've been having that conversation all your life. What's not part of that conversation, however, is something of much greater moment. It's something the Entreprenati know and live — far more significant than skills is the person wielding them.

Long before you reach the limits of your skills, you'll
come up against the limits of yourself.

Cultivate a burning desire to improve yourself. Don't stop working on your skills, but you must work just as hard—in fact harder — on building up the person who'll ultimately wield those skills.

Though a would-be warrior may learn the proper movements of the sword, yet he won't acquit himself well in battle if the man himself lacks the inner essence to carry out those movements with clarity of purpose, daring, grace under fire, fortitude, decisiveness, finesse, adaptability, faith, and deadly effect.

Become the person capable of achieving your dreams.

9

You're Sick

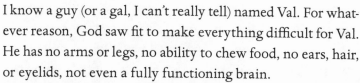

I know a guy (or a gal, I can't really tell) named Val. For whatever reason, God saw fit to make everything difficult for Val. He has no arms or legs, no ability to chew food, no ears, hair, or eyelids, not even a fully functioning brain.

Yet he manages to get by rather well, and, I dare say, even think and feel emotion (though I'm not sure about that one). Everything's a struggle for him, but he gets it done. And with no complaints. In fact, not only does he manage to sustain himself, but he even manages to achieve continuous growth. Moreover, he's easy to be with, nonjudgmental, content to do absolutely nothing for days on end, pure, and honest— despite his forked tongue.

Yes, he's a snake. A nine foot Boa Constrictor to be exact. No matter, the point's the same.

All too many people foolishly run around telling everyone who'll listen how difficult their lives are. They even wind up convincing themselves.

Some people actually do have difficult lives. They work a hundred feet under the ground in a coal mine. By the end of the day — each and every day — they're physically exhausted and have to scrub the coal dust from the pores of their skin. That is, if the mine doesn't blow up, collapse, or flood, which mines tend to do a bit more frequently than, say, the office you probably work in.

A penchant for complaining about the difficulties of one's life (real or imagined) is a symptom of a serious ailment of the human potential. It's an ailment that, if left untreated, will do grievous harm to your potential, if not kill it.

Another symptom of this ailment is blaming others. Your life's too difficult, you should be living on Easy Street, so it must be someone else's fault that you've not achieved this lifestyle. Your thankless boss, your backstabbing coworkers, your greedy partner, your unsupportive spouse, your lousy parents, the government, your mailman, God, Lady Luck— the usual suspects of a person whose potential is infected with the ERJ virus—Excuse, Rationalization, & Justification.

> *Unfortunately, the ERJ virus is naturally occurring in the human potential and most people never overcome it.*

The ERJ virus operates by blocking the human potential's commitment to results. Your potential loses its ability to see a simple truth—that people's lives (yours and others) are impacted by results, and if the right results evade us, then all the excuse, rationalization, and justification in the world won't change this fact. The effect will be exactly the same.

When confronted with an obstacle or anything that'll cause us discomfort, hardship, or sacrifice, it's natural to be of two minds—one that strives to overcome, while the other seeks a way out. "Hmm," sighs the ant. "This thing's a real bitch to move. Maybe I should try a different approach. I could get that silly old ram to help. Or ... maybe I should just pack it in. Heck, everyone knows an ant can't move a rubber tree plant." This second mind is anathema to the commitment to results.

Impact is born of results, not of efforts. Fair or not, that's just the way it is. So, the question shouldn't be "what can fairly be expected of me?" but rather, "how do I overcome?" Rarely is it impossible. It's a matter of resigning yourself not to be in a position of having to explain (to yourself or others) why you didn't do something you should have done, no matter how convenient the excuse, rationalization, or justification might be.

There are things you should be doing, but aren't. You know what they are. Chances are, you're excusing, rationalizing, and/or justifying those failings. The same goes for the things you shouldn't be doing, but are. Most people can't even see any of this, much less counteract it on their own. But this shouldn't come as a surprise.

It's an ailment, so you need treatment.

Treatment lies in enlisting the aid of others. Family, friends, colleagues, advisors and the like can help you become aware of your bad behaviors (of action and inaction) that you're excusing, rationalizing, and/or justifying, and they can help you stop those behaviors.

But they won't do this unless you specifically ask for their help. They may not notice your bad behaviors (of action or inaction), and even if they do, they'll likely consider it rude to point them out to you, much less to constructively work with you toward addressing those behaviors. You need to ask for their help.

Ask for it specifically and earnestly. Don't let any ego, stubbornness, fear of rejection, or lack of self-worth stop you.

*You're not too good, nor are you not good enough,
to seek and receive the help you need. You're just the
right goodness. Go for it.*

Tell your helpers the things you feel you should be doing, but aren't. Ask them to help you stop excusing, rationalizing, and/or justifying those failings. Likewise for the things you shouldn't be doing, but are. Ask them to keep after you, to hold you accountable.

After a while, you'll internalize the good behaviors (and externalize the bad), and you'll be able to continue on your own. Although you'll still want your helpers to be on the lookout to keep you honest, since the virus is never completely eradicated, and folks tend to relapse from time to time.

Take health and fitness for example. Everyone knows the right thing to do here. We know we owe it to ourselves and our loved ones to take care of ourselves. Yet many people don't, and they excuse, rationalize, and/or justify this irresponsible behavior by saying they'll get around to it, but at this point in their lives they have more pressing matters to focus on. More pressing than health? Hardly. But this demonstrates the power (and danger) of the ERJ virus. To overcome this, hire a personal trainer or engage a training partner. Treatment of the ERJ virus lies in enlisting the aid of others.

Realize you can't do this on your own; that's the first step. Next, get help. As the great philosopher Clint Eastwood once said, "a man's got to know his limitations," but, as Clint would surely agree, this doesn't mean a man must be limited by them.

10

Me Happening to Me

~~

A leaf rests on the forest floor. A wind blows and the leaf is carried away. The leaf has no say in what'll happen to it when the wind blows. But we do.

We build shelters to have our say. It's not a full say, of course, as the wind can still send shivers up our spine with its piercing howl, or even blow off our roof on rare occasion, but we definitely have a say in the matter. Even when we go outside, we wear clothes to deny the wind its full bite. This is how most people deal with the winds of life, but the Entreprenati have moved beyond this manner of reactive existence, and you can too.

> *People spend much effort shaping what'll happen to them when the various winds of life blow—they should spend as much shaping the winds that'll blow upon them in the first place.*

Winds are born of the interactions among weather systems. As in nature, each of us has our own personal weather system.

Is yours sunny in a sense that makes others smile, or that makes others see "sucker" written across your forehead?

Overcast hinting at a serious side, or betraying bitterness? Hot of a kind that burns excitement into relationships, or that burns all the fun out of them? Cold like crisp mountain air, or like a dead fish? Rainy as a springtime shower, or as the tears of a child robbed of her innocence? Dry as delightful humor, or as the parched throat of a traveler lost in the desert?

Yours is probably some combination of these and other types, but whatever it is, it is yours. You can change it. Or you can leave it be.

> *You are Mother Nature of your own weather system.*

At the center of this system is your energy — the energy you create through your perceptions, perspectives, thoughts, emotions, and actions. Circulating around this center is the energy of all the people and things you've attracted — the manifestations of your perceptions, perspectives, thoughts, emotions, and actions.

> *Your weather system is your "presence" in this world. It extends beyond your physical self. It operates even in places and at times where you're not physically present.*

The winds of life that'll blow upon you will be generated by the interactions among your system and those of others. This means you have three tools at your disposal in having your say on what these winds will be. It won't be a full say, but it'll be a say.

The first way you can have a say is by determining your own weather system. All too many people blame their circumstances for creating their crappy weather systems. This is convenient, but it's folly. Even innocents dragged off to war against their will who return horribly disfigured have been known to recover weather systems befitting a king. What could possibly be your excuse? Whatever your circumstances, you can always take charge of your own weather system. You can always take charge of your perceptions, perspectives, thoughts, emotions, and actions — the elements that bring about your system.

The second way you can have a say is in determining the other weather systems with which yours will interact. You can determine, at least to some extent, the people with whom you'll associate. You can also have some influence on their systems. When a sunny system meets a smoggy one, for example, at least some light is bound to shine through that funk.

The third way you can have a say is by altering your system in relation to others. You should be careful to maintain your authenticity, but this doesn't mean you can't adapt to your surroundings. Adaptation is good, so long as it springs from who you are, rather than compromises it.

So, next time you cast your gaze skyward and it looks grim, rather than reach for your umbrella, reorient your thinking to see it as cloudy with a chance of you.

11

Dem Bones, Dem Bones

~

The company was but a year old, barely turning a profit, and struggling to survive against fierce competitors. So Keisha figured it was a good time to hire a technology team and spend a million dollars over the next year in a high-stakes gambit to create groundbreaking software capable of catapulting the venture to the top of the industry. Not just any team, but one she planned to hire away from another firm—a team with no experience in her field, located a thousand miles away, led by a mad scientist type (Lucian) who she believed in.

It was a controversial position. Conventional wisdom dictated that the company wait until it was in a stronger condition before trying to pull off such a feat. If it ended in disaster, as so many major technology initiatives do, the enterprise might not survive such a blow at that delicate point in its embattled, fledgling existence. But Keisha believed they should go for it. Standing still isn't much of a strategy in the fast-paced business world, she thought, even if, and perhaps especially if, you're in a fight for your life.

But she stood alone. The company was getting by with its basic operations and could have purchased inexpensive off-the-shelf software if it wanted to gain some improvements. From Keisha's perspective, however, while generic technology could boost efficiency, it wouldn't significantly alter the firm's fundamental value proposition. Only proprietary technology held this promise.

The company's executives sought advice from high-octane consultants who laid out elaborate multiphase plans, replete with sophisticated PowerPoint slides, Gantt charts, and spreadsheets, detailing the form, timing and cost of each deliverable. Lucian, on the other hand, offered little more than psycho-technobabble, rambling musings the executives could scarcely comprehend.

He "assured" them, however, that he works "as efficiently as possible," and that his products are always "industry dominating," but he refused to provide any particulars, "explaining" that his ideas "present themselves" to him as he goes along, and so he couldn't know the form, timing or cost of the product until he created it. His style utterly confounded the executives, but Keisha still believed in him.

In an effort to turn things around, she scheduled a showdown between Lucian and the consultants, exhorting both sides to "take off the gloves." But Lucian was no match for the silver-tongued consultants. After mercilessly running rings around him, they brazenly asserted that hiring him would be "a recipe for disaster." They had common logic on their side, more than enough to carry the day with the company's executives.

Yet Keisha knew Lucian had the right stuff, but he just couldn't demonstrate it in a way others could see. She felt the company needed to go with the person who could get them to the right place, no matter how maddening the trip might be. So she had a heart to heart with the president.

The discussion got heated and the president wasn't budging. But then Keisha asked two questions that changed everything—she asked if his mind was open enough to see the possibility that the whole world might be wrong and Lucian right, and she asked if the president believed in her enough to accept her belief in Lucian. After an intense pause, the president yielded, but warned Keisha that "this guy better walk on water or there's going to be hell to pay."

With her victory in hand like a climber who just won the right to tackle Mount Everest, all Keisha had to do was hire Lucan away from the other firm and make sure he walked on water, which she did. The odyssey over the next year was as maddening as expected, but it did culminate in a system that truly was "industry dominating."

Keisha stuck to her belief in the face of biting adversity. She was willing to stand alone in her belief. To go to the mat for it. To act on it against all odds. But she didn't go against the grain merely to be a contrarian. Being the kind of person who's always for whatever others are against isn't a virtue. It's just being a pain in the ass. No, Keisha didn't pick this battle so much as it picked her. It was a calling.

In answering this call, was Keisha's course a wise one or was it utter foolishness that got lucky? It was neither, and it was both.

Boldness is the offspring of wisdom and foolishness.

As you can imagine, theirs is a stormy affair and their love child has quite a complex. On any given day, this kid could go either way. He could destroy your life as easily as he could take it to heights unseen. So, don't unleash him unless you feel thoroughly compelled to do so, unless you feel it in your bones. But if and when your bones do speak to you, listen to what they have to say.

The Tin

I put down Glith's chapters, scooched a bit lower in my easy chair, and looked out at the Paris night. The City of Lights it wasn't from the window of my apartment. The French blackness seemed no different than the one back in Chicago. As dark, as vast, as empty. And quiet enough to hear my bones speak, if they had anything to say to me. But they didn't.

I went to the kitchen and opened the fridge, but couldn't find anything I wanted in there. I was tired, but didn't want to sleep. As I cast about the apartment, my mind envisioned places to go—mostly bars or clubs at that hour—but none of those interested me. I sat on the couch and turned on the TV, flipped through the channels, but couldn't settle on anything, so I clicked it off. My brain started bouncing around thoughts and emotions, all mixing together into a mash that jammed up my head till it was about to burst. I felt the need to get the hell out, jumped up, and bolted to the closet, but when I opened the door, I couldn't figure out why. I stood there, frozen, staring into the closet. I didn't need a jacket. It was too warm outside. Why did I go to the closet? Something told me there had to be a reason.

As I tried to figure it out, my gaze drifted up to the top shelf and I caught a glint off the edge of an object otherwise beyond my view. I found myself reaching up there. My hands took hold of a metal box and brought it down. It was my old art supply tin. Tarnished and dented in the two decades since my seventh birthday, but still in one piece. And still following me.

I put it on the floor and popped off the lid. I lifted out one of my old sketching pencils, unwrapped the string to expose a fresh section and ran it along the underside length of my index finger. The soft charcoal melted at the warmth of my skin, laying down a thick black line from knuckle to tip. I rubbed the line with my thumb, blending away the blackness into a translucent sheen.

I placed the pencil on the floor and examined the other contents: my vine charcoal sticks, my willows, my white vinyl eraser, my kneaded erasers — one stretched out like play dough putty, the other still in its wrapper — my graphite pencils, my erasable pencils, my pastels, my red sharpener, my sanding block ... One by one, I removed each item and laid them all out on the floor. The inside of the box was still shiny. I could see myself in there, looking out.

After a while, I started placing the items back inside. One by one, they covered up the bottom, until I couldn't see out of the box anymore. I closed the lid and put the tin back in the closet. I didn't feel restless anymore, but I didn't feel at ease either.

I went back to my chair, picked up Glith's chapters, and returned to my reading ...

12

Friends in Low Places

~

Ask someone to tell you their weaknesses and you're liable to hear something like this: "Oh, I just get way too emotionally attached to my work ... I must drive my staff to the brink of exhaustion in my relentless pursuit of excellence ... poor darlings, I really should try not be such a hard-charging perfectionist."

Such nonsense is the norm because people are programmed to believe that weaknesses are criminal elements infesting their lives. That they should be targeted for assassination, and hidden from prying eyes until they've been suitably whacked.

Hmm ... so let me get this straight—in a world where success depends upon being remarkable at something of special value, you're supposed to be strong at everything, is that it? Rather than hone your skills in the area where you can shine, you should be improving in all areas, eliminating all those dreaded weaknesses?

Well, if you ever find yourself in a life where you have unlimited time and energy, then by all means go for it—work on all your skills until you're extraordinary at everything. Here on Earth, however:

*You better figure out what you're going to suck at,
figure it out fast, and suck at it proudly till the day
you die.*

You *should* suck at those things that don't significantly de-
tract from your core strengths. These "weaknesses" you
should wear as badges of honor in homage to your focus on
becoming a top performer. Yes, you suck at those things, and
that's just mighty fine with you. In fact, you should reclassify
them from weaknesses to key elements of your master greatness plan.

This mental shift, from embarrassment to pride concerning the "weaknesses" you choose to embrace as part of your
quest for personal greatness may seem esoteric, but don't
let this fool you. Most significant accomplishments aren't
achieved by one individual operating in a vacuum, but by
various participants, each playing a role in the overall operation. The trick is to fill each role with the player who can best
perform it. In this way, strengths are leveraged while weaknesses are minimized through the complementary dynamic
of the whole.

Most people will never become great at anything. So they
might as well work on their weaknesses. If you won't be
great, at least you can shoot for well-rounded. That's why
society programs you this way.

*Society's programming is for the masses, not the
exceptional.*

To the masses, it's common wisdom. To the exceptional, it's
shackles. You can accept this programming as common wis-

dom and keep your place among the common, or you can view it as shackles from which to be freed on your way to claiming your place among the exceptional. As always, the choice is yours.

13

Are You Chris

~

Raj knew Jamie to be a visionary and a winner. He heard this from many sources and saw it with his own eyes. Everything she touched at Colossus Corporation turned into gold, her people revered her, and they were richly rewarded.

When he learned she planned to start her own company, he asked to get in on the action, and she agreed he could join as a founding member of the new venture.

Raj was electrified, both for himself and to bring his best friend Chris onboard too. They'd always dreamed of working together in a hot startup and this seemed like just the ticket.

He told Chris all the exciting details, but rather than share Raj's enthusiasm, Chris was riddled with angst.

Chris worried that Jamie's success at Colossus might not translate into success at a small company. He also felt uncomfortable taking a pay cut. He'd be getting stock, but what if the stock value never materialized? In that case, he might work for a year or two at a reduced salary and never recoup his lost earnings. He worried that a young company might lack the staying power if it hit a rough patch. What would happen then? He'd be out of a job and without a severance package. These and other misgivings swirled around inside him, and the stress of it all caused him to suffer stomach pains.

Ultimately, Chris decided against taking the plunge.

Chris believed he had what it takes to enter the rough and tumble world of a new business venture, but at the moment of truth, when this belief was put to the test, turns out he's all hat and no cowboy.

Or is he?

Maybe this brand of adventure isn't a genuine calling for Chris, in which case, yes, he's no start 'em up cowboy. But there's another possibility — maybe deep down inside he really is meant for this, but something is blocking the expression of his authentic self. It's a critical distinction.

> *Funny thing about moments of truth — they reveal*
> *truth, but you can't always tell what it is.*

To one degree or another, life entrepreneurs, whatever their chosen adventure, live in a world where they're being pulled in multiple directions, putting out fires, ducking and weaving, flying by the seat of their pants, hoping to get more right than wrong, working to keep the wheels on their adventure and to keep it moving in a generally forward direction, without knowing for sure where this direction lies. It's a world where things are subjective and imprecise, where there are no answers, only judgment calls and educated guesses, and where stuff works or doesn't work in degrees and not in any absolute sense. That's why it's an adventure.

Whether one is to be a life entrepreneur of the small business stripe or any other variety, professional or personal, you must be willing and able to lead yourself through the precarious waters of your adventure.

If this brand of adventure is right for the authentic Chris, but something is stopping him from wading in, then he's not yet worthy of the challenge of his destiny. He needs to grow into the person who is.

But if it's not a true calling, then he's chasing a phantom. When you're reluctant to board the train you've been waiting for, you have to wonder if you really want to take that ride. If that ride isn't for him, he needs to come to grips with this reality. His is a different sort of adventure—he needs to hop aboard a different train.

What about you? Are you Chris? If so, which one?

14

Cut to the Chase

Ambiguous people should be shot on sight. No, that's too good for them. They should be strapped to a giant rotating spit and slowly roasted alive over a fire just hot enough to cause their skin to sizzle, then blister, and eventually bubble up into a boiling goo that melts off their bones, drop by drop, while they scream for the mercy of death.

Hey, that's just my opinion. Agree or disagree, you know where I stand.

Everybody's got to stand somewhere. Otherwise, you're nowhere. Want my opinion on that? I say don't go there — nowhere's no place to be. I say be anything but ambiguous. If there's a decision to be made, make it. And then get on with it.

Being ambiguous — whether in your decisioning or in your actioning — is weak and unattractive.

Why choose not to choose? When you're indecisive or tentative, you squander your power of choice. That's one of the most perverse atrocities you can perpetrate against yourself. If you think this overstates the self-destructiveness, think again.

Life is all about call and answer — you call, the
universe answers. It doesn't always answer the way

you'd like, but you get an answer. Then it's up to
you to make what you will of it.

But if you don't call, there will be no answer. Try working with nothing.

And if you babble a wishy-washy call, you'll get a wishy-washy answer. Muck begets muck. You wind up wallowing in it, flailing about in it. Not a pretty sight. Not one that'll attract the kinds of people, energy, opportunities, and resources needed for your success.

The amount of damage and lost opportunity caused by indecisiveness (not clearly making a choice) or tentativeness (not clearly acting on a choice) dwarfs that caused by erroneous choices and actions.

This isn't to say you must always take action. You can decide not to act. Doing nothing is often the wisest course. But you must make a clear decision not to act. That's not being ambiguous. The universe will give you an answer in response to that. You can then reassess the situation in light of this answer.

When you're ambiguous, it rots your soul. You may not realize it, but it truly does. You're cankered with angst and guilt.

You're in a diseased state of bondage—your spirit
is unable to fully express itself.

When you decide and act crisply, however, your spirit blazes in full expression. This radiates personal power, attracting the kinds of people, energy, opportunities, and resources needed for your success.

Now, you can never have perfect information about the current state of play. Far from it. Nor can you predict the future. So how can you be resolute amidst all this uncertainty? Some pretend the uncertainty isn't there. That's a mistake. You need to see that jungle in all its glory.

> *You then need to cut through it with the machete of decisiveness.*

As you have at it, the jungle will reveal things to you. Based on these revelations, you can reassess as you go along. Decisive doesn't mean inflexible. You should make course corrections, decisive ones.

But none of this will happen if your decisiveness machete lacks a sharp blade. In that case, little will be cleared, little revealed. The uncertainty will fester, and you will fester.

15

Screwed by Evolution

~

Ever parachute out of a perfectly good airplane? Break out in song and dance on a crowded street? Fast for a week?

Most people don't venture that far outside their comfort zone. Problem is, most don't venture out at all. Sure, you may claim to want to do such things, and that one day you'll get around to them, but that's generally a delusion.

Whether we're talking about busting out of our comfort zone or doing anything else that's scary or requires hard work, our most base impulse is to not want to do it. Unlike society's programming, here we're dealing with genetic programming.

We're hardwired, from prehistoric times, to not want to do stuff that's risky or difficult. Avoiding danger and conserving personal energy were matters of survival to the caveman. Today, not so much.

Primitive man hunted elusive prey with spears, while facing the threats of starvation, frostbite, disease without medical care, and man-eating dinosaurs. Now we worry about our 401(k) dipping in value, our kid coming home with a tattoo, or our air conditioner going on the fritz.

That's not to say modern life is free from serious danger; it's just that most of what we fear nowadays isn't really all that menacing, nor is there much need to conserve our personal energy. Yet we continue to shun risk, even if it often amounts to little more than the risk of embarrassment, and we continue to shun that which is difficult, as if conserving personal energy remained a vital imperative. Thousands of years after these base impulses have outlived their utility, we're still ruled by them.

> *Knowing this is crucial. But knowledge without action will get you only so far—to the inner edge of your skull to be exact.*

The key to making this knowledge fruitful is to understand that our inaction in the face of risk or difficulty doesn't flow from conscious decision making. It's a default mode. We don't realize we're failing to act. It happens automatically.

> *With nary a thought, we mindlessly forsake options that could hold wondrous promise. Even if this were a good way to survive, which it isn't anymore, it's no way to thrive.*

You can make a different choice.

You can choose to reject this outdated default mode. This choice is hidden, however, and a choice isn't a choice for someone who's blind to it.

In your subconscious, a loop recording is continuously being played out, instructing you to shy away from anything that's difficult or risky, without actually making a considered decision either way. The trick is to be self-possessed enough to recognize and get beyond this subliminal directive, so you can perceive the choice it was drowning out.

To be successful, you must exercise the ability to consider for yourself the potential virtues of facing difficulty and risk in any particular situation over the false siren song of noncognitive inaction. You must also be willing to venture outside your comfort zone — just far enough beyond your boundary to stretch it, but without becoming paralyzed, repeating this cycle toward perpetual incremental growth.

And don't forget to have fun doing it.

If that's all you ever do, you can be successful. But the Entreprenati have moved beyond the practice of incrementally moving beyond their comfort zone. They've permanently moved out of it. Left it behind. They've become comfortable in their uncomfortableness. This is far easier said than done. Pursuit of the Entreprenati arts isn't for the timid, nor is it likely to end in capture. Most who pursue these arts will fare no better than an aspirational lifelong journey of discovery and growth.

PART III

DANCE THE DANCE

June Meeting

As I leaned against the statue of King Louis XIV in *Place Bellecour*, watching some regulars play a game of *pétanque*, the French version of bocce, on a hazy June morning, I looked up to see Glith coming down *Rue Gasparin*.

Observing him enter and make his way across the square, I was gripped by the way he carried himself. It was striking. He seemed thoroughly infused by his surroundings yet completely apart. I realized he was always like this; I'd just never noticed it before.

He nodded as he approached. "*Bonjour*, Jesse."

"Fancy meeting you here," I said with a chuckle.

"Depends on your fancy."

"I guess it does."

"The next nine chapters," he said, handing me an envelope. Then he watched with amusement as two men argued over whose *boule* rested closer to the *cochonnet*. After a while, one man produced a ruler to settle the matter.

"So how are things?" he asked, turning his attention back to me.

"Not bad."

"Not bad? How about good?"

"I guess they're good. I mean being in France, that's great, it's just ... you know, this computer programming stuff I do at the bank ... it takes a lot of focus and ... I'm just having a little trouble with that right now."

"Trouble?" asked Glith, raising an eyebrow. "What sort of trouble?"

"I don't know. I like programming, but the kind I do now ... I'm just not into it."

"You must've been at some point; you chose it for your career."

"Well, sure, they said banking has lots of jobs, good pay, and you know ... seemed like the way to go. But I don't think it was ever right for me." I ran my fingers through my hair. "I mean, I'm not blaming anybody ... I just think something's missing."

Glith looked back toward the game. The players were all hushed as the next thrower, a man dressed head to toe in white, carefully studied the field, a dirt patch about the size of a double-wide horseshoe court, with the previously thrown *boules* arrayed around the *cochonnet*. "Notice how seriously they play," said Glith. "Even though there are no trophies or purses for the winners."

"I never thought of it that way."

Mr. White assumed the position, left foot planted in front, knees slightly bent, the metal orb held out just below eye level. With a bowler's swing of the arm, the deed was done, as the arcing boule smashed into the opposing team's best hope, knocking it to the edge of the court.

"Sounds like you have an interesting situation on your hands, Jesse. If you can't focus on your work, what'll you do?"

"It's no big deal. I can handle it for now. I mean, I can get my work done. But I'm going to start checking out other stuff too, that's all."

"Such as?"

"I don't know yet. I guess it's time to sharpen up that machete and begin whacking away at my uncertainty jungle."

Glith nodded, and looked back to the game. "Some of the players, like the last thrower, are called shooters," he said. "They clear the space for other players, called pointers, who aim right for the victory spot."

"Sounds like it's better to be a pointer."

"Not necessarily. Both have their place. Each player just has to decide which type he's going to be."

When the game ended, we walked up to *Rue de la République*, a major pedestrian thoroughfare lined with stores and eateries. "I'll look forward to hearing how your situation turns out," said Glith, as we slowly made our way along the crowded street.

"Me too, but now let's talk about your book. The last set of chapters was great. I learned a lot, maybe even more reading between the lines."

"That's wonderful, Jesse. The most meaningful truths can often be found in the unstated — if one searches for them there."

I thought I understood his point, and I was getting into his book, but I still wasn't sure what was going on. Was he just making up this Entreprenati stuff? Or was I missing something?

We walked only a short distance before Glith got tired and suggested we sit at a café. We relaxed, drank *Perrier Menthes*, soda water flavored with delicious mint syrup, and discussed what I'd read so far of his book. After an hour, Glith stood up, patted me on the back and nodded at the envelope he'd given me. "See what you think about those chapters."

"Oh, I will. You can be sure of that."

"By the way, remember when we spoke about being a shooter or a pointer?"

"Yes."

"Well, there's another option," said Glith, lowering his head down to whisper in my ear— "You could be the *cochonnet*." Then, with a wave, he went on his way.

Be the cochonnet? I thought. Would this be a good thing or a bad thing? Sheesh, what did it even mean?

When I got back to my apartment that night, I curled up on my couch and started to devour Glith's next set of chapters ...

16

Look Mom, No Hands

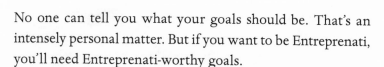

No one can tell you what your goals should be. That's an intensely personal matter. But if you want to be Entreprenati, you'll need Entreprenati-worthy goals.

Such a goal doesn't live in a place that's on any map.

But if you don't know where your goal lives, how will you get there?

When no map's available, we usually ask directions. Unfortunately, nobody else knows how to get there either.

Just as the landscape constantly changes in the physical world, so too does the landscape of the human world, only much faster. Yesterday's path isn't tomorrow's.

Even if someone else recently found a path, you still can't get there by tracing their steps.

> *Though you may walk the same way they did, you*
> *won't walk the same way they did.*

No two people walk the same. And, moreover, life paths are affected by how you traverse them. There's a continuous interaction between the person and the path that changes both, all along the way.

This doesn't mean directions aren't available. But it does mean that those directions can serve merely as rough guidance.

Some think they can plan out the voyage. They get disappointed in a hurry and usually quit. Others recognize their plan is just a starting point and must remain flexible and adaptive. They fare much better.

But what does it mean to be flexible and adaptive? Some say it means learning from bumps in the road and altering your course accordingly. This is true, but only scratches the surface of what's possible.

To tap into your fullest potential requires something far harder to achieve, and far harder to explain.

It requires discovery.

We're not talking about discovering the contours of the path. Remember, the path is changing (and you're changing) all along the way. We're talking about achieving a state of awareness in which you're tuned into this interaction between you and your path—its effect on you, and its effect on your path.

This is possible only on a sensing level, not a thinking level. Yes, you must think about what you're doing—but without controlling it fully. When your Thinking Self is in full control, your Sensing Self is pretty much in lockdown.

> *Only when you free your Sensing Self from the bondage of your Thinking Self can you achieve a state of awareness in which true discovery is possible.*

You can discover things that would never be visible to you otherwise. This is where your potential can make its greatest advances.

In any voyage, what you see is far less significant than what you don't. Most of the unseen will never succumb to human perception. Yet it's possible to steal glimpses of it now and then, not through your conscious sight but through your soul's eye — *if* you're in the right state of awareness. Being able to peer into the unseen, even for a fleeting moment, can propel you light-years into your future.

17

Unboulder Your Shoulder

~

It's bad enough that your success hides its whereabouts; must it also throw obstacles in your way? Well, in a word—yes.

It's not that your success wants to deny you its attainment. It just wants to ensure you're worthy of it.

So it lays out a suitable obstacle course. Seek a meager success, and you face an obstacle course that's a walk in the park. Seek a great success, and you face an obstacle course from hell.

First and foremost, an obstacle course requires maneuverability. The more challenging the course, the more maneuverability's required. But all too many people doom their own maneuverability, making it impossible to navigate their life's course effectively.

Knowing that life's an obstacle course, nature outfits each of us with a backpack at birth. You can wisely provision it with implements you'll need out there on the course (such as mindfulness, discipline, interpersonal skills, and coping mechanisms), or you can foolishly stuff it with crap you don't need—crap that'll weigh you down.

Sadly, most people load it with rocks.

The biggest rocks you lug around in your backpack are your fears—of failure, of success, of confrontation, of rejection, of embarrassment, and so on. These weigh you down the most, robbing you of the ability to navigate the obstacle course that is your life. You're condemning yourself to getting bogged down.

Let's face it, though, unpacking your fears is no mean feat. Once those rocks get into your backpack, they're mighty hard to dislodge. So you have to chip away at them. By forcing yourself to face your fears, you can chip away at them and remove them from your backpack in pieces. But you already knew that. What you don't know is this—

> There are a whole bunch of other rocks hidden in your backpack.

These rocks, though smaller, add up to a crapload of weight. The tragedy here is that they can be more easily removed, but you don't even know they're in there, so you don't make any effort to remove them. What are they?

> They're your hassles.

When you think something's a hassle, you've placed it as a rock in your backpack.

If you think it's a hassle to travel, work late, or learn something new—this mindset will bog you down. What if you thought nothing at all of hopping on a plane, even at a moment's notice, burning the midnight oil to solve an unexpected problem, or mastering any needed skill, no matter how foreign — wouldn't this free you to maneuver more fluidly in response to your life's ever-changing terrain?

The list of things you can view either as a hassle or as no big deal goes on and on. You can view things as hassles and thereby place them as rocks in your backpack, or you can view them as no big deal and thereby lighten your load — the choice is yours.

In fact, the Entreprenati have completely eradicated the entire hassle-mindset. They reject the very notion that anything could be a hassle. Indeed, they go even further — they embrace everything they encounter on their life's obstacle course as integral parts of their personal journey. You can do this too.

> *Life is the bee toiling to gather pollen, or it's the bee frolicking among the flowers — all depends on how you look at it.*

Traveling lighter not only increases your ability to react to whatever life throws at you, it also makes you happier. It enhances your enjoyment of your surroundings while en route to your destination. And, once there, you'll have more energy to celebrate your arrival, and to explore even further. Traveling light also decreases the risk of fatigue and stress-related injuries, both mental and physical.

Moreover, actively engaging in the challenge of reducing the self-destructive weight of your backpack is itself an enriching and rewarding experience. It makes you a wiser, stronger, more self-aware life traveler.

So—

> *Every morning, before venturing out into the world,
> take a moment to examine the contents of your per-
> sonal backpack.*

What rocks are in there? What fear-rocks will you chip away at today (by facing those fears)? What hassle-rocks will you toss out of there today (by ridding yourself of those counter-productive hassle-mindsets)? What maneuverability skills should be in there, but aren't, and how will you work toward acquiring them today?

18

Killing Time

In 1972, when Henry Kissinger visited Beijing on a diplomatic mission, he got to talking about history with China's Prime Minister, Zhou Enlai. At one point in the conversation, Kissinger asked Zhou for his opinion on the historical significance of the French Revolution of 1789. Zhou replied: "It's too soon to tell."

Some say patience is a key ingredient of success. Others profess just the opposite, that one must pursue success like a lion hunting down its next meal. Yet others attempt, in various ways, to harmonize this contradiction between patience and hungry pursuit.

> *The Entreprenati know a different truth — that there's no contradiction.*

Slow and steady may win the race in a children's fairytale, but being slow and steady for its own sake is nothing to be proud of. Unfortunately, far too many people confuse their lack of zest and inactivity for the virtue of patience. No, success isn't something one comes upon while sauntering along on a leisurely morning stroll. It's something that must be captured through vigorous quest.

Any moment when you're not thrilling to the chase
won't be a moment when success will be yours.

The harmonizers observe, however, that even the lion stalks its prey slowly at first, patiently waiting for the right time to pounce. Nice try, but no. You see, unlike gazelles, life's opportunities don't mosey about the meadow, grazing on grass, waiting for you to sneak up on them. No, they're on the run themselves. Why? Because while you're sitting around deluding yourself into thinking you're exercising the virtue of patience, others are hot on the heels of those opportunities.

Moreover, though the lion may seem mostly still during the initial stalk, the reality is quite the opposite. The lion's faculties are racing into hyperdrive, furiously collecting and analyzing the scents, sounds, and movements all around. What's the herd doing? What of her companions? How's the grass reacting to her paws as she eases them down ever so softly and to those of her companions as they each inch along? Is the grass acting as a loyal silent partner or is it betraying them? Are any other predators entering the arena? Any other intruder alerts that might send the herd running in any particular direction? Any of the prey seem weak or inattentive? The lion's heart pounds. Blood gushes through her veins. Her muscles twitch wildly as she struggles to control her breathing. Her eyes bulge, adrenaline surges.

Would this describe you in your patient moments?

The process of accomplishing any goal involves phases. The lions, for instance, must first locate their prey, then strategically position the members of the hunting party, then stalk, then pounce, then chase, then catch, then finally bring down and kill.

> *True patience is the capacity to engage in each phase for the optimal amount of time before advancing to the next, and to sequentially move through all the necessary phases in this manner until the goal is accomplished.*

Engagement, not sitting around. Sticking with each phase as optimally required, not jumping the gun. Staying the course, not trying to skip phases, not letting up, not quitting.

19

Bringing a Knife to a Gun Fight

It's out there. Smack dab in the way to where you want to go, composed of solid rock and monstrously dimensioned, as if silently screaming to all comers: NONE SHALL PASS.

Buster the Bruiser tries to ram through it. But the wall gives as good as it gets, leaving Buster battered.

Perry the Persuader tries to convince it to yield, but it's like talking to a wall.

Mary the Manifester tries to vision it away. "Nice try," says the wall, "but I'm wise to your secret."

Crafty Chrissie tries to find a way around it, but runs into a minefield and gets blown up. R.I.P. C.C.

Freddy the Friender tries to become the wall's buddy, but gets the stone cold shoulder.

Wanda the Worker tries to climb over it, but all her efforts don't amount to a hill of beans.

Which brings us to Versatile Vick ...

He sizes up the wall and realizes he better get the scoop on this bad boy before deciding on his mode of attack. So he writes a note on a piece of paper, places it in a can, and tosses it over. It's a note that asks— "How did you get past the wall?" He then curls up with a good book while he awaits a response. A few hours later, the can comes flying back over. Inside is his answer: "On Tuesdays, the wall leaves for the day to visit its mother in the next town." Based on this intelligence, our man adopts the waiting game approach.

Next Tuesday, after the wall scampers off to see mum, Versatile Vick trots across to the other side. When it comes to overcoming life's obstacles, one size definitely doesn't fit all.

> *Unfortunately, most people develop only one technique and then try to apply it in every situation.*

Maybe it's the first one that worked for you and you've been clinging to it ever since. Or maybe it's just your personality to be a bruiser, schmoozer, or some other type of self-defined one-trick pony. Whatever the reason, it's bad news. All these techniques and others can be highly effective — but only under the right circumstances. You can't turn a bolt with a screwdriver, nor a screw with a wrench.

Another problem with being a one-trick pony is that other people can read you like a book. They can anticipate your thrust, ready their parry. They can also throw hurdles in your way that they know are immune to your one technique. In these and other ways, they can manipulate you.

> *Being predictable isn't a smart strategy.*

Yet even if you do develop a wide arsenal of obstacle-clearing weapons, they'll be of scant utility unless you learn which ones to deploy in which scenarios. You must become skilled at gathering intel on the potential barriers you might face, then reading the situation as it unfolds, and then selecting just the right weapon to take out the particular blockage that rears its ugly head.

Some would never dream of acting like Buster the Bruiser, but there are times when you just have to take off the gloves. Likewise, some can't see how any obstacle could ever be defeated through manifestation, and that's their limitation—they can't see it. Where, for instance, they see a dream-wrecking tsunami up ahead, maybe you see a really big wave, one you can catch and ride to glory. The power of human consciousness to alter reality is profound, but only if you develop this power—and know how and when to unleash it.

And so it goes for all the techniques mentioned above, as well as others. In the right hands, under the right circumstances, they can move mountains. Limiting your repertoire means you probably won't be the owner of those hands, won't be the one moving those mountains.

20

Stay Tuned

~

Asked about the psychological significance of his cigar smoking, Sigmund Freud, the father of psychoanalysis, once replied—"sometimes a cigar is just a cigar." In fact, that's true for most people, but it wasn't for Freud and it isn't for the Entreprenati. Freud saw repressed emotions in all things. The Entreprenati see future possibilities.

> It's part of the Entreprenati way of experiencing their world through full purposeful engagement with their environment.

Take an Entreprenati chef, for instance. As she's experiencing her world through full purposeful engagement with her environment, inspiration will abound. She'll spy a flower, and see a colorful new vegetable medley. Caress the weave of a fabric, and feel a new rice texture on her palate. Catch the scent of a man's cologne, and smell a new brew of earthy spices. Listen to a symphony, and hear the resonance among a new combination of dishes.

Are you experiencing your world through full purposeful engagement with your environment? You look, but what do you see? Touch, but what do you feel? Listen, but what do you hear?

Now, if you're thinking this doesn't apply to what you're doing, that it applies only to creative endeavors, you're totally right and completely wrong. Why? Because every enterprise is susceptible to creativity. In fact—

> *Only those who rise to the level of artists in their*
> *pursuits can ever hope to become Entreprenati.*

An artist is one who expresses him or herself through any medium. There's no medium that's immune to self-expression.

Consider Wall Streeters. The artists among them turn on their lights and see the possibility of trading electricity. They get a whiff of pollution and smell the possibility of trading greenhouse gases. And so it goes ... at the top of every field, there are artists ... and the best of them experience their world through full purposeful engagement with their environment.

> *This requires a fusion of passion and mindfulness.*

Without passion, any "engagement" would be of a limp-wristed variety. Without mindfulness, your passion is the child deprived of toys.

> *Mindfulness means awareness of what's happening*
> *in your inner world and in the outside world, and*
> *the interaction between the two.*

This requires, first and foremost, that you be present—

> *Here & Now*

Not there or then. Here and Now. Got it?

Imagine what you could achieve if you lived your life through full purposeful engagement with your environment. Behold deafblind Helen Keller, renowned thought leader and international activist, she published twelve books, delivered lectures in thirty-five countries across five continents, helped found the American Civil Liberties Union (ACLU), and was awarded the Presidential Medal of Freedom. Think about it. Imprisoned in darkness and silence, yet she engaged with her environment with shining and thundering intensity. So what's stopping you?

Charisse

Chained to a vender's cart a few yards from the park bench where I sat, he struck a menacing presence. Hunks of muscle tightly packed over thick bones, eyes that see but don't tell, and rows of teeth at the ready, yet it was his facial wrinkles that defined him most.

As my fingers swept feathery strokes of chestnut to gradually deepen the crease looping inward toward the bridge of the dog's nose from his eyelid, I envisioned how to blend it into the folds of skin rippling down his permanently angry forehead and then flow it around his muzzle and hanging jowls. Just a little more shading would produce the right effect. A little more here. A little more there.

I felt a warm breath on my ear. I turned my head and my nose almost touched hers. *"Ces't un beau dessin,"* she said, as she sat back. She'd apparently been sitting right next to me, leaning over my shoulder.

"Thank you," I said, not knowing what her words meant, but knowing they sure felt good.

"Oh, you are American."

"Yes."

"Your drawing is beautiful."

"Thank you, again," I said, but I was thinking about how beautiful *she* was, like Vermeer's Girl with a Pearl Earring, the Scarlet Johansson version.

"I did not intend to disturb you. I was enjoying your work."

"No, no, you're not disturbing me, definitely not, but how long have you been sitting here?"

"Since you started on the ears."

"Wow. Sorry, I didn't mean to ignore you."

"It is okay. I was admiring your devotion to your subject."

"Well, he's easy to be devoted to. He's so majestic."

"He is a *Dogue de Bordeaux*. I think you Americans call him a French Mastiff."

"That's right. You know your dogs ... my name's Jesse, by the way."

"They call me Charisse."

Charisse? Hmm ... a suspiciously good name for a vision. Was I dreaming or was I really being chatted up by such a hottie? I must not have wanted to know the answer, because I never did have an urge to pinch myself. My urges were otherwise occupied anyway.

"Are you studying art? Is this why you are in Paris?"

"Studying art? No, no, it's just a hobby."

"You have a hobby drawing giant dogs?" she asked with a devilish smile.

"That's *one* of my specialties," I said, winking. "But I draw everything ... I mean I used to draw everything ... this is actually the first thing I've drawn in years."

"Why did you stop drawing?"

"I don't know."

"Why did you start again now?"

"Did anyone ever tell you that you ask a lot of questions?"

"Everyone who knows me."

I definitely wanted to be one of those lucky people. I spent the rest of our brief time together trying to accomplish this, but didn't get far. Charisse didn't talk much about herself before saying she had to go. I barely mustered the courage to ask her out, and was thrilled when she said yes. We made a date for the Louvre. She was surprised I hadn't gone there yet. I was too.

21

Join the Club

⌒

Leonard's company sells a unique type of self-cleaning twee-
zers (patent pending). He ships them to wholesalers by the
thousands. He's been in business for over a year and none of
his customers has ever failed to pay any of his invoices. That's
a 100% collection history. Too bad.

He's losing money this way.

If he'd loosen his credit policy a bit, to allow for a small
number of unpaid invoices, he'd make more money.

Here's why. Say he sells a thousand orders a month, at an
average price of $5,000 per order, and makes a 20% profit
margin. This translates into a million dollars of monthly
profit (1,000 orders, times $5,000 each, times his 20% profit
margin). Now let's see what happens if he loosens his credit
policy to accept a couple hundred additional monthly orders
from less creditworthy customers, some of which will default—say a dozen. This means he'll get 188 paid new orders
(200 new orders minus the 12 that go unpaid), generating
$188,000 of extra profit (188 paid orders, times $5,000 each,
times his 20% profit margin), but he'll also incur $48,000 in
credit losses (12 unpaid orders, times $5,000 each, times his
80% product cost). This comes out to $140,000 in net extra
monthly profit ($188,000 from the paid new orders minus the

$48,000 of credit losses from the unpaid ones). His monthly profit would increase from $1,000,000 to $1,140,000.

As you can see, loosening his credit policy would boost his profit by 14%. Leonard would earn $1.68 million more every year by allowing himself the "mistakes" of shipping to some customers who ultimately default on their invoices. The same is true with the way you conduct your life.

If you think it's great not to make any mistakes,
you're seriously mistaken.

Understand, we're not really talking about overcoming your fears. Sure, it's scary to ship product to buyers with imperfect credit. But not much. Leonard isn't afraid of a few unpaid invoices. No, his shortcoming lies not so much in fear, but elsewhere.

Nor are we talking about learning from your mistakes. That's ultra-important, but it's another topic altogether.

Nor are we talking about intelligent risk-taking. That's also a different topic. There's no real risk in accepting relatively small-sized orders from a controlled number of customers with imperfect credit. Even if a significant percentage of these customers default, Leonard could simply tweak his credit policy in the following month to fine-tune the process. It would be different if Leonard were selling multibillion-dollar satellites, where one payment default could sink him. But that's not the case here, and it's not the case in your day-to-day life either.

As you go about your daily activities, one of the factors that influences your behavior is your view on mistakes. All too many people make the mistake of thinking they shouldn't make any. This suppresses their self-expression, and this, in turn, suppresses their performance (and their happiness) — that's what we're talking about here.

To avoid mistakes, you're forced to engage in self-inhibiting behaviors. You take on less challenging projects, work in an excessively cautious way, deal with others in an overly circumscribed manner, take too long before speaking up (if at all), set your bars too low, and so on.

> *The cumulative effect of these self-imposed constraints in limiting your performance over the course of your days is staggering.*

So, in addition to losing out on the benefits of intelligent risk-taking, of overcoming your fears, and of learning from mistakes (none of which are the topic of this chapter), you also retard your self-expression—and that, my friend, is the unkindest cut of all.

Allowing yourself to make mistakes can dramatically boost your self-expression, which can open a floodgate of achievement.

> *So, rather than take false pride in your lack of mistakes, you should join the "I Wish I Hadn't Said or Done That Club."*

Be a proud member of this club. Make no mistake about it, membership in this club has its privileges.

Many factors can cause you to hold yourself back—your fears, laziness, lack of self-reliance, inability to endure pain, analysis paralysis, rationalization, and so on. Your mistaken belief that mistakes are bad is also one of those factors, a big one.

Mistakes are neither bad nor good. If your mistake frequency is too high, that's dangerous. But if it's too low, you're moving through life too cautiously, too unassertively. You need to pick up the pace. You need to bring the heat.

> *While you may think a zero tolerance for mistakes is a tough stance, it's really a weak one. You're not actualizing your true potential, not fully utilizing your gifts.*

Don't hold your reins too tightly out there.

22

Life in the Fast Lane

⁓

Racecar drivers live at the boundary between chaos and control. They pilot their vehicles on the ragged edge of dynamic equilibrium, barely holding on to the ground as they barrel through turns, slingshot past competitors, dodge spinning cars, and evade flying crash debris—all at warp speeds. Think we can learn something from them about piloting our own adventures at the hyperfrenetic pace of life?

Hop in, buckle up, grab the wheel, and mash down on the throttle, as we blast onto the track to see what lessons we can discover out there.

When you focus right in front of the car, things flash by in a whirring blur of confusion and you're overwhelmed by a sense of speed and danger. But when you look far ahead, you can see things approaching, you have time to process them, and your faculties are freed from the debilitating grip of sensory overload.

To go fast, you need to know where to go slow. If you enter a turn too fast, you'll be forced to compromise your speed through the rest of the turn, which will reduce your speed down the ensuing straight. The modicum of advantage gained at the entry ultimately costs more than it's worth. Going in a bit slower allows you to come out much faster.

Regularly glance at your rearview mirror, so you can see who might be gaining on you. Don't let it distract you, but do consider what changes you might make to avoid being overtaken.

When things go awry, our natural instinct is to reach for the brake. But it's generally more effective to keep your foot on the gas, make steering adjustments, and switch gears on the fly. Slowing down usually isn't the best corrective action.

Keep your eyes moving, so you look at nothing and see everything.

To go fast on the track, you must operate the controls smoothly in the cockpit—quickly, but never abruptly, and always deliberately (even if subconsciously at times).

Monitor your instruments in order to continuously measure your performance. A good subjective read is vital, but can be misleading. You also need objective metrics.

Allow awareness of the dangers to sharpen your concentration, but not to hinder your thought process or actions.

Use your mind's eye to examine individual things, while keeping sight of the big picture, and always driving toward the desired destination.

Recognize that before we can reach the limits of the racecar, we must first transcend our own limits, and we can only do this by pushing ourselves beyond our comfort levels—but not so far as to become paralyzed.

When you exit out to the pit area, unbuckle your five-point harness, take off your crash-rated helmet, unzip your three-layer firesuit, and debrief with your crew, you should realize that the racecar driver boldly faces the perils on the track, but doesn't do so foolishly and doesn't do so alone. He uses the latest safety equipment, researches each track and each competitor, trains relentlessly to identify and prepare for the challenges he'll face on race day, and works seamlessly as an integral part of a dedicated team.

23

Do I Know You

~~~

Business books brim with tales of swashbuckling pioneers who set sail for glory under impossible conditions only to miraculously prevail against all odds. Or at least the business equivalent of such a fantastic voyage.

Take the story of Fred Smith, for instance, founder of Federal Express. In college, he wrote a paper about starting a company to go mano a mano against, of all things, the U.S. Postal Service. His professor promptly told him he was nuts and that his idea would never work. Did this deter our hero? Of course not. Fred went out and did it. Not only that, but when he ran into financial straits early in his quest, did this derail him? Of course not. He flew to Vegas, bet everything he had, and won big—fueling his continued battle against his mammoth rival. And we all know he went on to slay that leviathan and emerge a god among men.

Well, whether or not such stories are actually true, they make a point. Any success worth capturing lives out on the edge. Many folks lust after it from afar, at a safe distance. The only way this can ever work is if luck intervenes. But luck doesn't have the time to go out there and get your success for you. Luck's got a lot on its plate. It might lend a hand, but only if you're willing to step out to the edge and get its attention, and prove yourself worthy of its assistance.

Yet it's one thing to expect luck to do the job for you (that's a nonstrategy); it's quite another to disrespect luck, to escapade out to the edge like a jackass, tempting luck to throw you into the abyss—that's a bad strategy, a very bad one.

So what's the difference between pushing your luck and thumbing your nose at it?

> *The answer lies in perception, understanding, analysis, planning, decisioning, and execution. These six things.*

It all begins with perception. As explored in other chapters, however, looking is easy, while seeing is hard. Those chapters provide some tools that might help you better succeed at seeing what it is you're looking at.

But even if you achieve this perception, there still remains the challenge of understanding. That's what this chapter is about. People often make the mistake of "thinking" they understand risk, but that's impossible.

> *You can't understand risk on an intellectual level—only on a gut level.*

It's common knowledge, for example, that when the cash runs out for a business owner, the game's over. But all the theory, case studies, and spreadsheets in the world can't do justice to the real life experience of staring into the faces of desperate employees clinging to jobs you can no longer maintain, angry creditors clamoring for payments you can no longer make, indignant customers demanding services you can no longer provide, and terrified loved ones looking to you for salvation from the financial inferno engulfing your family—all like ravenous animals struggling to feed off the carcass of your tortured soul.

My purpose isn't to scare you, but to drive home the importance of truly knowing the things that can kill you in each variety of endeavor. For a business, lack of cashflow is the leading cause of death. Business startups should ensure they have sufficient capitalization, or at least a way to get it that doesn't involve a trip to a casino. In other pursuits, different assassins loom. Unless you've personally come up against these grim reapers, you can't truly know them.

Yet, being stung isn't the only way to know the wrath of a wasp. An analogous experience, like being bit by a dog, can serve as a suitable, if imperfect, substitute (okay, a very small dog). Or seeing someone else get stung can be nearly as meaningful. The key is to experience it up close and personal. This is why life experiences are so paramount.

If you lack the precise or analogous experience, direct or indirect, you should look to an advisor, mentor, coach, partner, colleague, or friend who has such experience.

> *As always, though, you must possess the self-aware-*
> *ness to know what you know and what you don't.*

Every adventure is different—know how to get killed in yours.

24

Eye of the Tiger

Once you truly understand the risks involved, the next order of business is to analyze the risk/reward calculus. Consider the nature and magnitude of the risks versus the potential rewards, their probabilities, the factors bearing upon those probabilities, the alternatives, the ways to mitigate the risks, to manage the risks, to monitor the risks, to deal with contingencies, and the costs (money, time, and other costs). If your analysis suggests in favor of a go-forward decision, the next step will be to create a plan. After that, it'll be time to make your decision. If you decide to green-light the plan, then your challenge will shift to execution.

Hmm ... so here we are chatting about risk analysis, planning, decisioning, and execution in a calm, detached manner, as if considering a possible trip to the grocery store. But while food shopping isn't usually a death-defying act, here we're dealing with something that can kill you (figuratively speaking anyway). So how can this discussion be at all realistic without recognizing the fog of fear that must necessarily enshroud any such contemplation of risk?

In the face of risk, it's natural to be fearful. Only an insane or otherwise mentally disordered person wouldn't feel this way. And we all know fear can be debilitating. It can block you from taking on challenges and can severely diminish your performance in the ones you do take on.

That's why some believe it's a liability to be aware of risk in the first place. But this is folly. Yes, there are those who do things blind to the risks and succeed, even wildly so, but the vast bulk of them wind up as road pizza. The vast, vast, vast bulk. We tend to hear only about the precious few who succeeded, and this creates a warped sense of the prospects of such a stupid approach.

Which brings us back to fear. Even a fear based on an accurate read of the risk can be debilitating. Worse, many exhibit overblown fears. For some, it's because they've been burned in the past (once bitten, twice shy). For others, it's the exact opposite — they're overly afraid of the unknown (the devil you don't know is scarier than the one you do). Overblown or not, how should one deal with such fears?

Well, the word "courage" might spring to mind — but what does this really mean?

It certainly doesn't mean failing to understand the risk. In fact, it's only courageous if one proceeds with such understanding.

Nor does it mean not fearing the risk. That's impossible. Once you understand the risk, this understanding will manifest itself as fear. Depending on the person and the situation, the level of fear will vary, but it will be present.

Nor does the answer lie in pretending the fear isn't there. No, it's there, and it won't be ignored. The answer lies in transformation —

> *True courage is the transformation of fear into focus.*

If you have confidence in your ability to perceive, understand, and analyze the risk, and your ability to properly engage in the planning, decisioning, and execution that flow from it, then you're halfway there toward transforming your fear into focus. This half of the transformation is fueled by belief in yourself. It requires you to develop expertise in these abilities *and* to recognize your possession of this mastery.

The other half of the transformation is fueled by belief in something outside yourself. Without this second belief, the transformation will be incomplete, some fear will remain, your focus won't be its sharpest.

So, what is this belief in something outside yourself, this belief that completes the transformation of fear into focus, solidifying your courage? It's a belief in a universal truth. A universal truth that must become one of your own personal truths.

> *Do everything you can (in the perception, understanding, analysis, planning, decisioning, and execution) and the universe will take care of the rest. Things may not turn out how you had hoped, but they'll usually turn out well, and always as they should.*

Do you believe this? The Entreprenati do. This belief, coupled with belief in yourself, can transform your fear into focus.

When you perceive and understand the risks you face on your adventure, properly perform your analysis, planning, and decisioning, and then embark with full belief in yourself and in the universe as your partner, then no fear will remain, only focus—and *that* is true courage.

Any other form of courage is incomplete or something else masquerading as courage, such as ignorance, foolishness, lack of self-worth, desperation, rage, or any number of other such imposters. There's a lot of counterfeit courage out there.

PART IV

EMBRACE & BE EMBRACED

July Meeting

Glith and I next met up at a tiny eatery on *Place des Célestins*, the square in front of the *Théâtre des Célestins*. Since Glith told me his "secret" some months ago, all our meetings were down here in Lyon. He'd apparently stopped making his business trips up to Paris.

The flowers were in full bloom all around the square on that sunny afternoon and I was enjoying the birds singing all around us. I remember thinking there must be more birds in France than in the states, because I didn't much notice their concerts back home.

"I like this place," I said. "It looks like something out of a history book."

"And what a history it has," said Glith. "In fact, this square is located on land once owned by the Templars. They had a command post here until King Philip IV had them arrested in 1307. After that, the Célestins established a monastery and later this magnificent theatre." Glith paused and stared at the theatre for a while. "For such a grand old lady," he finally said, "She looks mighty fine."

"Yes she does," I replied, but I was thinking Glith didn't look so fine. He was thin and pale, and his movements seemed labored. I was worried. It must've shown on my face because when he turned his attention back to me, he waived me off with a hand gesture and a smile ... "But enough about ancient history," he said. "Last time we met, you told me your heart isn't in banking and you were going to explore other areas, to see where your true passion lies."

"I said that?"

"That's what I heard you say. Did I hear wrong?"

"No, no. You're right. I guess I just wasn't thinking about it that way."

"Any developments?"

"Well, yes, I *am* following my heart — straight to Charisse that is," I said with a chuckle. "We started seeing each other a few weeks ago and it's going great."

"Ah, that explains it. You seem to have a newfound gusto. Now I know why."

"You know part of it," I said, winking. "The perfumed part. But I also found my gusto professionally."

"You've gotten over your funk at work, is that what you mean?"

"Nope," I said, with a smirk, relishing that for once it was Glith who was left wondering.

Glith sat back in his chair and crossed his arms. "Okay, enlighten me."

"Three letters — CGI."

"*Code Général des Impôts*, the French tax code?"

"Not even close. I'm talking computer generated imagery. That's what's got my name written on it ... written all over it ... just took me a while to see it ... I guess I was thinking too much, when I should've been feeling more instead."

It felt strange mouthing those words. Like someone else was doing it, while I wished it were me. I'd awakened my truest creative passions and discovered CGI as the best way to express them, but this was the first time I actually said it out loud.

"Computer generated imagery," said Glith. "Animated movies, special effects. That's quite different from banking."

"It sure is. They use sculpting software to create digital 3D objects, like cars, buildings, people, creatures, asteroids, and entire planets, to craft their shapes and visual properties, like textures, colors, transparency, refraction, and reflection, to add the lighting, winds, and other elements of their surroundings, the viewpoints, distances, and angles, and the movements to bring it all alive."

"Sounds like you have it all figured out."

"Not really. I know what I want to do, but not how to make it happen. There's so much to learn. Can I learn it on my own or do I need to go back to school? Where and how can I get in? Will they even accept a retread like me?"

"Even better, sounds like you have some exciting stuff to figure out."

Exciting, definitely. But daunting as hell. Although I didn't let on, I actually felt completely overwhelmed. In the span of a few short months, I'd rediscovered my art, fallen for a dangerously beautiful woman, decided to change my career, and ran into a swarm of new emotions. Part of me wanted to slow it all down. A part of the old me. The new me knew to keep my foot on the gas, switch gears on the fly, and make steering adjustments as I barrel along. And if I make mistakes, so be it. In theory anyway.

It was exhilarating to think like this, but, truth be told, I wasn't so sure I could really pull it off.

We spent the rest of the evening talking about what I was learning from his book. Later, as we left the restaurant, Glith handed me the now-familiar envelope. "Enjoy the next installment," he said, as he turned and walked away.

Back at home, I tore open the envelope, pulled out the next set of chapters, and began to read ...

25

Dream a Little Dream for Me

~

Everyone's born a dreamer.

For a few, their early dreams come true. These are the rock stars, professional athletes, astronauts, movie makers, and other products of a child's imagination.

For most of us, however, the whimsical dreams of youth eventually give way to adult dreams — whether to earn the respect of parents, the love of a life partner, the blessing of children, a trade or profession that strikes the mind as a noble calling, an avocation that makes the heart sing, or whatever other aspirations quicken the adult soul. These dreams range from simple to grand, fulfilled to works in progress, dormant to forgotten.

Most people focus on trying to give flight to their own dreams. Yet there are those who practice the art of helping others give flight to theirs. These are the wing whisperers.

The Entreprenati are wing whisperers ... and by helping others realize their dreams, they also realize their own.

Consider Henry Ford, founder of the Ford Motor Company. In the early 1900's, he invented the assembly line manufacturing process. Its enhanced efficiency enabled him to raise his workers' daily pay from $2.34 to $5.00, which was revolutionary. Thousands were freed from the chains of poverty, inspiring them to pursue their American Dream.

And the dreams didn't stop there. His company produced the Model T, a car affordable to the common man. In one year alone, nearly two million were sold, empowering the masses to join in a collective dream of modern mobility that swept the nation.

Ford also pioneered a franchise system through which the ambitious could create their own dealerships, resulting in individually run distributers throughout the country and on six continents. These proud new business owners were able to fulfill their dreams, and to become wing whisperers themselves.

Ford's company also generated profits, fueling the dreams of its investors as well.

And countless other enterprises sprang up to become parts suppliers, gas stations, repair shops, road builders ... the dreams rolled on and on.

Henry Ford certainly was a wing whisperer. And by spurring others to achieve their dreams, old Henry lived the grandest one of all.

But, you say, you don't own a company, and you don't even hold a high position in the one you work at. You're just a middle manager at Behemoth Corporation. So you can't be a wing whisperer. Nonsense, of course you can. The four people you manage have dreams, don't they? Even if you manage nobody, there are colleagues, customers, vendors, and others with whom you interact, or could interact. All these people have dreams. You can always play a role in helping people reach their dreams.

This also applies to your personal life. Do you have kids? If you're a good parent, aren't you the central figure in nurturing your children's discovery and ultimate fulfillment of their dreams (and those of your parents, as well as your own)? What about friends and others in your life? Don't they have dreams you can help them attain?

In their own individual ways, many people are wing whisperers. Many others could be, but make a different choice. A wing whisperer can help thousands inspirit their dreams, and in doing so, can also live his or her own. Yet it needn't be thousands. One will do. It's not about numbers. It's about a state of mind—and actualization of this state of mind.

26

Come Hither

~⌒~

Shit attracts flies. Prey attract predators. Flowers attract pollinators. And so it goes in the world of attraction ... which, by the way, is our world.

> *The Entreprenati understand that you don't get*
> *what you want in this world—you get what you*
> *attract.*

Succeeding in different pursuits requires you to attract different things. Identifying those things and learning how to attract them is critical. Most people do neither.

Some folks try to grab the things they need for success. But their success is limited—because grabbing attracts resistance. Others try to buy what they need. But the most vital ingredients for success aren't for sale. True loyalty, for example, can't be purchased. It can only be attracted.

Attracting people, the right kinds of people, as well as the right kinds of energy, opportunities, resources, and other wonderful stuff is the key to the kingdom, as is not attracting the wrong kinds.

Others are attracted to you for their own purposes, never yours. Even if they're attracted by a desire to help you, or to defend you, or simply to be your friend, this still means they're motivated to satisfy this desire of theirs. So, you'll attract those whose desires are satisfied to one extent or another by associating with you.

Let's say, for example, you want to attract high performers to follow your lead in a particular adventure. Well, the high performers you seek are themselves seeking something — they're seeking to blast off toward the heavens. So, it's simple:

> *You need to look like the rocketship that's going to get them there.*

Each person has his or her own heavenly destination. For Silicon Valley types, it's bleeding edge technology. For the wizards of Wall Street, it's high finance and mega deals. And so on and so forth. High performers will be attracted to you if they believe you can lead them to their desired destinations.

> *True leaders know they are, first and foremost, all about inspiring people's beliefs.*

This manifests itself in different ways in different leaders. For some, it's charisma. For others, it's a compelling vision charged with the power of its inevitability. There's no single recipe. Each leader inspires belief through his or her own unique vehicle. However you make it happen, people must believe you have what it takes to create and maintain an environment for their success — that you're their rocketship.

But you must be real. We're talking not about manipulation, but radiation. Magnetic radiation.

Other people's desire is up to them, but whether or not you look like the object of that desire is up to you. Your genuine attitudes, perspectives, priorities, ethics, and values, as expressed through your honest words and behaviors, determine whether or not any particular type of person feels attracted to you.

> *If you believe you're attracting the wrong kinds of people, then either you're not radiating your true authentic self or else you're wrong about who you really are.*

If, for instance, you're attracting those who are down on themselves and their prospects for a good life, then you must look like someone who'll wallow along with them in their self-pity or self-loathing, or someone who'll otherwise join them in their self-defeating thoughts, feelings, or behaviors, or maybe even someone they can tear down to make themselves feel better about their own perceived inadequacies. So which is it—are you really such a person, or are you failing to radiate your true authentic self?

Look around you. Do you see flies? If so, guess what you are—or at least what you look like to others. Similarly, if you see predators circling, you must look like an easy mark. What you want to see is pollinators. Then you'll know you're attracting healthy associations that are mutually beneficial. The flower gives of its sweet nectar, and the nourished visitor shares the love.

As you work to improve yourself, look around you to see what you're attracting—not only in terms of people, but also energy, opportunities, resources, and other things. If it's trending toward the right stuff, then you're on the right track. Otherwise, you have to question who you really are inside or how you're radiating yourself to the outside world.

27

The High Performance Memberless Organization

~

Have you built an organization through which you can achieve your goals, or are you merely part of other people's organizations, helping them achieve theirs?

All of us are part of other people's organizations.

The question is — do you also have your own?

If you're sheep, the answer is no. You're spending your life helping others enrich theirs.

If you're like most — more than pure sheep, with at least a little wolf in you, then you have an organization, but it's only moderately concerned with helping you achieve your goals. More effective people have organizations with a greater focus on furthering their aspirations. The Entreprenati have killer organizations.

We're not talking about a traditional organization, like a corporation.

We're talking about your own personal organization.

Consider a successful venture capitalist, athlete, or author. Each has his or her own personal organization.

The venture capitalist may or may not be at a large firm (most aren't), but in any event, this would be only a part of his personal organization. He also has a gaggle of accountants, lawyers, and others who feed him a steady flow of quality deals; he has a raft of senior executives around the country whom he can call upon to serve on boards of directors or in management positions at his portfolio companies; he has business school professors who supply him with the brightest students to work as analysts during school and after graduation, and so on.

The athlete has a strength coach, a flexibility coach, a speed coach, a masseuse, training partners, a dietician, sponsors, and other members of her personal organization.

The author has an agent, publisher, editor, graphic artist, website designer, publicist, and so forth.

Those who operate in these organizations often do so on an informal or part-time basis. The accountants and lawyers who refer deals to the venture capitalist operate informally in this capacity. The athlete's coaches may also train others. The author is just one of his agent's many clients. No matter. Each has built his or her own personal organization, and whether the people comprising it function formally, informally, full time or part time, function they do.

> *The organization exists and operates with a high level of collective impact in behalf of all its members, but especially in behalf of its "leader," even though it might not be considered an organization in the traditional sense.*

The word "leader" is in quotes because this person wouldn't be viewed as the leader of the organization by its

members. In fact, the members often don't even view themselves as part of this person's organization. The venture capitalist's referral sources, for example, view themselves as part
of their accounting or law firms.

So, we're talking about building and leading an organization whose members don't even recognize they're in it, much
less that you're its leader.

Build your organization of non-members, and lead your
non-followers to achieve great things.

28

Clowns to the Left of Me, Jokers to the Right

~

Charismatic, over the top, and larger than life, Lorenza owned every moment. The founder of her own logistics company, she was a force of nature and all her employees worshipped the ground she walked on. Yet despite her outsized stature and big talk about expanding her business nationally, even globally, the company's growth stalled early and never did catch fire. It did well but never became anything more than a local player.

The problem — a hundred people sharing one brain.

An organization's growth will be severely stunted if its members are merely appendages of the leader's body. This is the opposite of high-leverage leadership. Unless the members think and act for themselves, the organization won't get very far. This is true whether we're dealing with a company or your own personal organization.

Lorenza surrounded herself with weaklings. This is an all too common malady. The "leader" feels threatened by strong performers, so she attracts lightweights. For this type of leader, her assured charisma is a display designed to mask her insecurity. Afraid of appearing threatened, she projects the illusion of unshakable confidence. This is a subconscious behavior, as she's also presenting the illusion to herself.

Lorenza told everyone what to do and how to do it. She monopolized all aspects of leadership. Although she created the appearance of empowerment, it wasn't real. She let others hold the gun and wave it around, but only she could pull the trigger. And because her people had no autonomy, they never felt responsible for anything.

This attracts people focused on obedience, rather than performance.

Yet, Lorenza lamented their weak performance. This contradiction shouldn't be a surprise, however, as this sort of leader lacks the self-awareness to recognize that she is the alpha and the omega of her own problem.

> *Are you Lorenza? Are you afraid to surround yourself with strong performers?*

If so, you're not on a path to the Entreprenati.

But even if you do surround yourself with stars, you're still on the wrong path if you're not confident enough to let them shine. Holding down your charges enslaves not only them, but you too.

> *If you make yourself a warden, you also place yourself in prison.*

Free your people to shine and you free yourself as well. Foster their self-reliance and you free yourself from having to provide them with all the direction. Foster their inner drive and you free yourself from having to keep your foot firmly planted on their backsides.

Consider Ferdinand Magellan (1480–1521), known as the first explorer to lead a successful attempt to circumnavigate the planet. He earned this distinction despite the fact that he himself didn't complete the voyage. He was killed midway, but his crew carried on without him. And they did this in the face of hellish adversity. Of the approximately 250 men who set sail on five ships in 1519, only 18 completed the trip and managed to return in 1522 on the single remaining vessel. Not only did his crew not disband after his death, but they took the initiative on their own to continue the voyage around the globe. Magellan was the type of leader who inspired such epic self-reliance and inner drive in his "followers." History appropriately recognizes him as the leader who achieved all this through those he turned into self-leaders.

As with Magellan, your greatness will flow from attracting top-flight people and bringing out the best in them. By creating and maintaining an environment where high performers can flourish. By unlocking the greatness in others.

How do you do this? Simple. Provide them with a compelling mission, measurable objectives, clear roles, access to the necessary information, processes, authority, and resources, an effective reward & accountability system, a culture that encourages and manages intelligent risk-taking, open communication channels, and appropriate controls, and then clear away any obstacles or distractions that might impede them, monitor their performance, and provide feedback as the adventure unfolds. Piece of cake, right?

29

Cornucopia

The recently deceased don't make good customers, vendors, partners, or associates. They won't attend meetings (even if beverages and food are served), won't buy anything from you, won't tap their contacts for you, won't help you raise money or gain any other resources you might need. And they don't get any more useful later when they start to rot and stink.

Going after customers, vendors, partners, and associates like a hunter pursuing prey will doubtless end in this wretched way.

Farmers do things differently than hunters. They plow the soil for fertility, strategically plant the right variety of seeds in the right places, supply nourishment, protect the crop, and ultimately harvest what they've cultivated. They grow their own future.

But all too many people don't grow their own future. They hunt. They try to get the most out of every interaction and every transaction, while paying or otherwise giving as little value as possible in return. They stalk their prey in search of the "payoff"—to make the sale, close the deal, acquire the information, obtain the access, or whatever else they hope to walk away with. Problem is, you don't walk away. You remain in the same world as the person you just bagged.

Yet, unlike a hunter of beasts who guts his quarry,
your human quarry will gut you.

Rather than create allies and admirers who are excited to be around you, who look forward to being involved in your pursuits and sharing in your achievements, you create zombies. This spreads diseased energy that denies you benefits, assistance, and opportunities that healthy energy would attract.

In sales, for example, those who churn customers through the system are on the wrong path. They figure they'll just grab everyone they can, sign them up for the product or service, and move on to the next target. They're looking out only for what they (mistakenly) believe is in their own interests. They aren't considering if the product or service is right for the customer. In other words, they're just out there hunting away.

This creates a sickly business. The churned often feel burned. Even those who wind up benefiting in some way from the product or service can see how heartlessly they've been treated. The atmosphere becomes poisoned.

While the hunter enjoys the thrill of the kill, it's a shortsighted pleasure. The farmer, far more proactive in sowing the seeds of his own success, reaps a richer bounty.

When you respect and nurture people, rather than kill them, you grow allies and admirers. This creates a world of wonderfulness around you in which all things are possible. This is the way of the Entreprenati.

30

In the Company of Yourself

～

You are absolutely marvelous to be around. Or at least that's what you think. Why else would you spend most of your time with people just like you—and you know you do.

So, there you are, all wallowing around in the mud of your sameness. No newness. The you of today looking a whole lot like the you of yesterday. The you of tomorrow? Well, let's just say growth isn't in the forecast.

Don't underestimate the profound impact your associations have on you, positive and negative. Many fail to recognize this. Even as they work to build themselves up through education, training, and other means, they often sabotage their development by failing to suitably upgrade their associations.

> *The aspect of your environment that plays the biggest role in shaping you is the collective influence of the people you spend time with.*

That's why it's vital to actively manage your associations—actively to the point where it becomes a central focus of your personal development program.

Want to eliminate your bad habits? Spend less time with people who reinforce them. Want to improve yourself in a particular area? Spend more time with those who excel in it. This applies to every aspect of your life — even (and especially) your most fundamental qualities. To cultivate a more positive outlook, a broader consciousness, a greater zest for life, you should be with people who look on the bright side, see the other sides, and embrace them all. In fact, this "should" is really a "must" — because you are or will become who you *choose* to be with. Full stop.

> *You can transcend your environment, but not your choices.*

If you want to think in new ways, seek out new opportunities, live a different quality of life, but you choose to remain in the same old environment, your wants will wither. Not because of your environment, but because you chose that environment, even if by default. A nonchoice is still a choice. You won't achieve your wants if they're inconsistent with your choices. To upgrade your life, you must choose to upgrade your environment. This means, first and foremost, choosing to upgrade the people who comprise it.

Your associations exist across various groups. You may have one or more work-related groups, one or more groups of your own friends, maybe another group you share with your spouse, another at the gym or in some other clubs or activities, and so on. These groups may range in size from a dozen or more down to just you and one other person.

Each of these groups, regardless of size, can play a pivotal role in shaping who you are — in your professional life and in your personal life — and who you may or may not become.

Don't make the mistake of thinking about this in
terms of being with those who have wealth, connec-
tions, power, or influence.

Of course such things can be extremely beneficial, but we're
talking about something even more significant here—the
impact others have on you as a person. If, for instance, you
spend time with those plagued by a scarcity or fear mentality,
this blight tends to infect your being.

Most people suffer the consequences of hanging with folks
like themselves because, quite simply, they don't recognize
it's even happening. Worse, many think it's great if they're
the best among their cohorts. Fools.

To get to the top, you need to head straight for the
bottom.

If you're at the bottom of a group, you benefit most by the
associations, as you're lifted up by the others. If you're at the
top, the others are dragging you down.

The trick is to spend less time with those who'll drag you
down and more with those who'll lift you up. Problem is,
those are the ones trying to avoid spending time with people
like you—they don't want you dragging them down.

To counteract this, your challenge is to figure out a way
to be of interest to them. Develop some special knowledge,
skill, connection, talent, ability, or attitude so you'll be viewed
as bringing something to their party.

Not only do you benefit from the direct interactions with
those in your improved group, but those outside your group

tend to identify you with the quality of your group. Run with a better crowd and you're tagged with a better brand, which can do wonders toward attracting the kinds of people, energy, opportunities, and resources needed for your success.

Upgrading your associations may require you to completely end your participation in one or more groups and/or to create one or more entirely new ones.

So, go ahead and aim straight for the bottom and don't stop till you get there. As you surround yourself with people who have the qualities to which you aspire, they'll lift you up. Actually, you'll lift yourself up.

31

Handle with Care

～

Some live to share their fire, others to burn you with it.

As with any destructive element, it's crucial to identify the type you're facing and to respond accordingly.

One type, for instance, is the victim who suffers a tortured childhood and spends the rest of his days getting even with the world, whether through hostility or treachery.

Another type is compensating for insecurities. They feel small or inadequate in some way and are trying to make up for this by "getting over" on others, overtly or covertly.

Then you have the folks who get inebriated by power and stumble into wickedness.

Yet there are those who employ ill means as a calculated tactic, either all the time or selectively. This can take the form of manipulation or bullying.

And there are the alpha wolves. Unlike the tortured souls, compensators, and drunks, who are all struggling with their demons, or the calculators who are deliberately misbehaving, the alpha wolves are simply aggressive by nature. It's not a tactic they turn on and off, nor the product of internal strife. It's who they are.

Not all destructive people are so obvious about it. Consider, for instance, your leeches. They're on the job nine to five, sucking blood from their hapless colleagues in every

field. They're also out there masquerading as customers, vendors, friends, and others out to drain you dry. It's often hard
to notice they're sucking your blood because they cleverly
secrete an anesthetic into the bite to block you from feeling
it until after they have their fill and slink off to digest.

For the tortured souls, understand you're actually dealing
with the temper tantrum of the troubled child within. Let
this guide your interaction.

For the compensators, consider how firefighters seek
to cut off a fire's fuel. Here, that fuel is the compensator's
insecurity. Work to alleviate this and you'll quell the fire it's
feeding.

For the power drunks, consider how firefighters use
"tactical ventilation"—openings and fans to create pathways
that draw the fire in desired directions. Aim to direct the
drunk's projections of power to your advantage.

For the calculators, throw water on them by making them
realize their ways won't work with you. They've made a calculation that you (or the situation) can be manipulated or bul-
lied to their advantage, so you need to correct their erroneous
math. Set them straight, subtly or not so subtly, depending
on the circumstances. Unlike the others, they're misbehaving
based on rational thought, which means they'll alter their
course if they discern it's counterproductive.

For the alpha wolves, understand they'll eat you alive if
they smell fear or weakness. The way to gain their respect is
to show some teeth. Don't go overboard; just let them know
you're nobody's lunch. They'll still be tough, but they'll come
to the table, rather than circle for the kill.

For a leech, the recommended method for removal is to
gently break the seal of its sucker, and then you can flick it
away (resist the urge to violently rip it off, because this may

cause it to regurgitate its stomach contents into the wound and the vomit may carry disease). To prevent leeches from attaching to you in the first place, be on the lookout for colleagues who appear slimy, who have blood stains ringing their mouths, or whose jaw shapes match the bite wounds on your colleagues' throats. Vigilance is the key.

Not all who appear destructive actually are. Some are just gruff in manner, not in spirit.

Yet others are merely having a bad day or going through a rough patch and it's getting the better of them. Try to see beyond the temporary ghoulish handiwork of their plight, to reach the perennial within.

Even a good chap can turn bad if jammed in a tight spot. If, for example, you're negotiating with someone who's under pressure to make the deal come out a certain way, imagine yourself in his shoes and work toward a solution that takes into account his particular predicament.

In all situations, be sensitive to a person's need to "save face" — especially when her boss, spouse, client or others are involved whose opinions matter to her. Rather than trap her in a corner, leave her an escape route that doesn't appear as such, allowing her to back down gracefully.

But how do you know which variety of damage monger you're facing? How do you know if it's one of the tortured souls, compensators, power drunks, calculators, alpha wolves, leeches, face-savers, rough-patchers, tight-spotters, or some other type of destructive person? Begin by doing your homework; research the players and the field of play. Armed with this intel, observe the game as the student of animal behavior I hope you've become, and take your best guess. This dictates your starting point. Then adjust as you go along. It's a human experiment.

But sometimes the experiment goes awry. You try every-thing, but to no avail. Some folks are just plain FUBAR. Well, just as some fires can only be extinguished by blowing them up—firefighters literally blow them up with explosives—you do the same. Threaten to pull the deal off the table, call the person out, go over his or her head, or deploy some other transformative countermeasure. It needn't involve shock & awe. It can usually be done indirectly or otherwise diplomati-cally. The most potent bombs are often those that never detonate.

When you do cross paths with a destructive person, work hard to learn from the encounter. Learn from what you did right and from what you did wrong. These are among the richest growing experiences you'll ever be gifted.

> *Use these gifts to develop tools of sensitivity, per-*
> *suasion, advocacy, negotiation, finesse, maneuver,*
> *and, yes, confrontation.*

The Entreprenati possess all these tools, and they are equally adept at utilizing any one of them as each situation warrants, any series of them in any sequence, or any combination all at once.

If you learn how to handle damage mongers, not only can you prevent them from harming you, but you can also win some powerful allies. And don't forget that the worst people can often push us beyond our normal limits, bringing out our very best.

32

Believe You Me

～

You tell your five-year-old daughter it's bedtime. She tells you it's a special occasion. She's not buying what you're selling. Who's doing the selling now?

Sure, you can snap at your little girl and angrily order her to bed, or you can calmly but firmly say she must follow your rules, but in either case you'll have blown the communication. She'll remain unconvinced there was good reason to end her day and she'll get the wrong message (to be intolerant, mean, or despotic). Better to explain why going to bed would be a healthy choice, or would allow her to enjoy more of the next day, or some other valid reason, and why it really isn't a special occasion.

You communicate for a reason. Sometimes to convince, but always to gain buy-in. Even when you merely wish to express yourself, this still means you want others to buy into your self-expression. To understand it, to find it interesting, to deem it legitimate in some desired way, or to buy into it in some other sense. But—

While talk is cheap, being heard isn't.

Being heard means something. It's a great honor to be deemed worthy of being heard. This must be earned.

Your audience will test the mettle of your communication before buying into it. Their antennae will be extended and twitching away as you communicate, trying to detect any distortions (intentional or subconscious), ulterior motives, hidden agendas, or other disqualifying defects.

When you and your message pass this antennae test, when your audience feels you're genuinely interested in conveying what you sincerely believe, their ears will open. Even those who don't buy into your communication right away may do so later.

Yet even those who do make a good faith effort at expressing their honest truths often blow the communication by becoming fixated on gaining the buy-in. That's a mistake.

It makes you a prisoner of your audience's mind.

You've climbed inside and you're pushing buttons, hoping to find the buy-in button. The button that'll satisfy *your* fixation. But people don't like you crawling around inside their heads. Their only thought is to get you out of there. That's the opposite of listening to you.

To free your audience to really hear you, don't try to push their buy-in button. That's their job, not yours. This isn't to say you shouldn't try to read your audience and tailor your approach. Because you should. But—

Don't sell. Instead, create space that allows others to buy.

When you respect your audience's right to make their own buy-in decisions, your communication can't fail, as its proper purpose, to further build your world of healthy energy, will have been accomplished.

Whatever communications you offer, release yourself from the responsibility for your audience's reaction. Immerse yourself instead in the passionate pursuit of sharing what's in your heart. This will free your spirit and your audience will sense this. When your spirit is free, you can soar. When you soar, others are drawn to take flight with you.

33

When Push Comes to Shove

In 1519, Captain Hernán Cortés, sailing under the Spanish flag, landed his fleet in the New World, on the shores of what's today known as Mexico. After some nasty skirmishes with Aztec warriors bent on eating their heads, the captain got the sense that maybe his men were having second thoughts about the whole conquesting thing. It seems his men had grown rather fond of their heads, at least so far as keeping them attached to their bodies was concerned. So, legend has it, Cortés burned his ships. With no way out, he figured his men would be more focused on the task at hand. A choice between victory and death does tend to concentrate the mind.

That's the difference between followers and leaders — followers need drivers and leaders are in the business of delivering them.

Effective leaders can gauge the types of drivers their followers need. The captain determined his men needed the ultimate driver, and he delivered it in spades.

But before you can develop the ability to deliver drivers to others, you need to be driven yourself. You must be internally driven.

Internal drive can derive from myriad sources. Some folks grew up poor and are driven to escape their lot. Others are driven to prove themselves more worthy of their parents' admiration. Yet others may discover a calling and become driven by this passion. The list of driver geneses goes on and on. Each driven person is driven in his or her own way.

If you have such an internal drive, you may be on your path to the Entreprenati. That's definitely a requirement. There are no Entreprenati among the cattle.

But what if you don't have an internal drive? Is all hope lost? Are you forever doomed to followerhood? The answer is no. It's possible to develop this drive. Hard as hell, but it's the only game in town if you ever hope to become a leader, ever hope to become Entreprenati.

One way to play this game is to intentionally place yourself in a situation where powerful external drivers will operate to propel you along. Jump off a cliff and thereby create the drive to learn how to fly. In other words, you quickly internalize the external drivers. Or you don't, and you quickly get dead.

Many have had great successes with such an all-in strategy. Many more have lost everything they hold near and dear. It's boom or bust. Feast or famine.

For some people, in some situations, that's the way to roll. Those who start capital intensive businesses, for example, often have to lay everything on the line. Raid the savings account. Max out the credit cards. Mortgage the house. Sign personal guarantees beyond their net worth. Yes, this does tend to concentrate the mind. There are pros and cons to such an approach, of course, and it's not for everyone, but, in the final analysis, it's pretty cut and dried—victory or death.

But what if you're interested in something that doesn't entail such a high-stakes gambit? Want to become a top real estate agent? A marathon runner? A chef? These and many other pursuits can be commenced at minimum cost, and can be abandoned early on at minimum pain. Therein lies the rub.

A low price of entry and exit means a low price of failure. Most people are driven much harder by fear of failure than by desire for success. Still worse, there's actually no possibility of failure. Rather than fail, you simply move on. It's cost- and pain-free. Sounds good, but it's actually the kiss of death for most people.

Now, this isn't a problem if you're passionate about your pursuit. In that case, you're internally driven by this burning desire and don't need an external driver, such as the Aztec warriors lusting for your head or the threat of financial ruin faced by the small business owner. But many who turn out to be successful at something weren't all that passionate about it when they started out. Like a romantic relationship that blossoms into a great love — first there's a spark, then an ember, a small flame, and ultimately an inferno.

Yet early on, the small flame is delicate. Many people unwittingly allow it to flicker out, frittering away any chance they had for success.

Their shot never has a shot.

But it doesn't have to be this way. You can build synthetic drivers to bridge the gap until you develop real drivers.

Start by creating concrete goals, writing them down, and announcing them to your colleagues, friends, and family. This demonstrates commitment and generates expectations, which are synthetic drivers. Next, track and keep your people updated about your progress (or lack of it).

These goals must be written. Otherwise, they're merely wishful thinking.

They must be concrete. Otherwise, you won't have a clear direction to drive towards.

They must be announced. Otherwise, no external drivers will come into play.

You must track and keep your people updated about your progress (or lack of it). Otherwise, the external drivers will be weak and short-lived.

To further strengthen the drivers, write down measurable objectives regarding each goal, announce them, and track and report your performance (or nonperformance). The operative word here is "measurable" — you must be able to determine whether or not you're achieving these objectives. This must include deadlines (or target dates or milestones, if you prefer more positive nomenclature), as Father Time is the ultimate taskmaster.

To strengthen those drivers further still, ask others to hold you accountable for your performance against your objectives. Depending on how seriously you can get these folks to function as enforcers, this can dramatically strengthen the drivers.

Just as each goal should be associated with the objectives you'll accomplish to reach that goal, so too should each objective be associated with the action steps you'll take to accomplish that objective. Write down those planned action steps, announce them, and then track and regularly report your steps, nonsteps, and missteps.

In totality, this is a three-tier structure. On top, there are your goals. In the middle level, there are the objectives below each goal. At the base, there are the action steps below each objective. Then all you have to do is drive up that structure by taking those steps, which accomplishes their associated objectives, which brings you to your goals.

To create a complementary set of synthetic drivers, engage in meditation visualizing your success, coupled with affirmations—verbal and written. Pick one or more consistent times each day for this (each and every day), schedule this on your calendar (in writing), and stick to it. Here, again, it can be extremely helpful to enlist others to hold you accountable.

To further reinforce these synthetic drivers, identify early wins that seem highly possible (i.e., easy), and focus on achieving them, no matter how small. Early positive results are key in establishing the synthetic drivers. Don't underestimate the power of early wins. Proactively seek out those little jewels.

Early on, while your synthetic drivers are fragile, it's critical to identify the obstacles that might set you back, and to steer clear of them. You'll tackle those challenges later, after you've cemented your synthetic drivers firmly in place. Don't underestimate the danger of early setbacks. Proactively scan the horizon for those deadly icebergs.

These synthetic drivers are precursors to internal drivers or to nothing. Eventually, if the pursuit is right for you, your little flame will start to roar and you'll develop internal drive. Otherwise, other pursuits beckon.

— PART V —

LOOK AT THINGS DIFFERENTLY

August Meeting

The next time I met up with Glith, it was for dinner at one of his favorite restaurants, a small place, only about five tables, located on a quiet street in Lyon, with no sign out front. Glith introduced me to the owners, a sister and brother — she did the cooking and he attended to everything else. They seemed so glad to see Glith.

Although he was in his usual high spirits and tried to put on a good face, Glith looked terrible. We didn't talk much during the meal.

We were enjoying our after dinner drinks when Glith lit a smoke, inhaled, and hacked out a wicked cough.

"Are you okay?" I asked. "You've looked a lot better, you know."

"A lot better than what," he said, cracking a faint smile, as he crushed out his cigarette in the ashtray with a trembling hand.

"You have to take care of yourself," I said. "You're part of my personal memberless organization and I need you in top form."

Glith raised an eyebrow and grinned. "Okay, my friend, I'll do my best to pull my weight ... for as long as I can."

For as long as he can? What does that mean? But before I could pursue it, he changed the subject.

"Last time we spoke, you said you were going to find a way to break into CGI."

"Umm ... yeah, that's right ... sure, I've been getting to know people in the field, learning what each of them does, building relationships. I even struck up a good one with the owner of a graphics company, and I've been letting them know how interested I am."

"And ... have they been receptive?"

"Yes and no. I mean, they seem like good people, but I get the feeling they think it's too much of a stretch ... you know, that maybe I should be looking at something closer to home, in financial services." Although I didn't say it, I wondered if the "they" didn't also include a part of me.

"Is that what you're going to do?"

"No, I've already done that ... pick something because it's practical, rather than what I really like, what I can really get into." This much I knew. Whatever my doubts were about how I was going to do it, I knew there was no turning back.

"So how will you make the move?"

"I don't know yet, but I'm going to buy one of the 3D graphics software packages and learn how to use it. It'll be expensive and take a ton of time, but I think I should go that first step, invest in myself and show I'm serious. You know, lop that beast's head off."

Glith nodded approvingly, as he lifted his glass to sip some of his beloved *Eaux de Vie* — water of life, a special type of pear brandy that was his favorite *digestif,* as he called it.

"I'll also widen my net. Get more involved in the CGI community, join the trade associations, participate in their groups, attend their events."

"Sounds exciting, keep me posted on this new adventure of yours," he said, placing his glass back on the table and standing up. As always, he left some of his drink over, and some of his food. I once asked him why he did that, and he said he preferred to decide for himself how much he would drink or eat, rather than have the restaurant decide it for him.

"I'll definitely keep you in the loop," I said, as we left the restaurant. "And also Charisse. This way, you can both hold my feet to the fire. I think that's important."

"Funny you should say that. During the Crusades, inquisitors applied flames to the feet of the accused until they confessed or died."

"Huh... not quite what I had in mind, but I get the idea. Thanks. I guess."

We spoke for a few minutes longer, as I walked Glith to his building. He seemed unsteady. I was very worried, but didn't say anything because I knew he didn't like to talk about it and I wanted to respect his wishes.

Later, as I made my way to the train station, I thought about Glith's condition. Should I have said something? Was there anything I could do? I also thought about that Entreprenati stuff. I still had a problem believing it, but started to think maybe I was the problem. Just because I couldn't see it didn't mean it wasn't there.

Back at my apartment, I opened the envelope and dove into the next set of Glith's chapters ...

34

What's Your Problem

~

Give people skyscrapers and they'll complain about slow elevators.

That's what happened a hundred years ago when buildings began reaching great heights. The elevator ride took much longer, which made for grumpy riders who demanded faster service.

The building owners pressed the elevator companies for solutions. Some recommended the development of more powerful motors, coupled with improved pulley systems capable of handling the forces of the increased speed. Other companies advised buildings to add extra sets of elevators. But all these approaches were prohibitively expensive.

The problem seemed insurmountable. People were demanding faster elevator service, but the buildings couldn't afford to provide it. So, they did what anyone would do in that situation — they installed mirrors. And, of course, this solved the problem.

What?

How could mirrors make the elevators faster? They couldn't. Good thing this wasn't the problem.

The problem was that people were bored.

After the mirrors were installed in the lobby, folks would arrive, press the button, and start admiring themselves in the mirrors, adjusting their collars, patting their hair, straightening their ties. They'd also steal glances at others, while looking to see who might, in turn, be checking them out. And all this furtive peeping didn't stop on the ride up—because mirrors were installed in the elevator cars too. Boy, I tell you, there's a lot of action going on over at the mirrored elevators these days. The life of the elevator rider will never be the same.

Before then, they had nothing to do but stare at the walls waiting for the lift, and then do the same on the ride up. The trip seemed to take forever. So they complained about slow elevators. The building owners then went about trying to solve the problem of slow elevators. Thus framed, the problem seemed insurmountable. Properly framed as a problem of boredom, however, it was easily solved. In fact, the riders thanked the owners for "speeding up the elevators."

> *Your success in life depends on the quality of the*
> *answers or solutions you craft to the questions or*
> *problems you believe your life poses to you.*

Over the course of your days, you'll spend an enormous amount of time and energy crafting those answers and solutions.

> *But what's of greater importance is to make sure*
> *you perceived the right question or problem in the*
> *first place.*

Many people misperceive life's questions and then poorly answer them. They're living lives based on bad answers to the wrong questions. Guess where this leads?

Smarter people do a better job answering the questions, but still may be answering the wrong ones.

Life doesn't speak English, so the questions it poses often get lost in translation.

Not only must you ensure you're correctly perceiving life's questions, but also that you're asking the right questions of others. This is imperative because how you frame the question or the problem often dictates the answer or the solution.

A man asks a priest if he may smoke while praying, and the priest answers — "No, during prayer one should be completely devoted to honoring God." A man asks a priest if he may pray while smoking, and the priest answers — "Of course, one should never resist the urge to honor God at any time."

What questions are you endeavoring to answer? Are they the actual questions your life is posing to you or are they mistranslations? What problems are you endeavoring to solve? Are they the actual problems you face or are they imposters? What questions are you asking of others? Are they designed to elicit the answers you seek?

35

In or Out

~

"Some guys are admired for coming to play ... I prefer those who come to kill." So said the sportsman Leo Durocher. Now, Leo wasn't a nice guy. He believed in winning any way you can as long as you can get away with it.

> *The Entreprenati come to play—and they come to kill. They don't follow the rules—but they don't cheat.*

Each variety of endeavor involves its own form of gamesmanship. Some participants believe certain aspects of the game are overly aggressive, unfair, or otherwise inappropriate, and they refuse to play those parts. Not only is this wrongheaded, it's also unethical.

We rarely play the game for ourselves alone. We almost always do so as part of a team or on behalf of others. All these people hold stakes in the outcome of the game and are expecting their participants to play to their greatest collective advantage. That's part of the bond among the stakeholders.

> *Anyone who's unwilling to play the game all out, based on personal sensitivities or otherwise, is unfit*

to discharge the duties of this bond, and commits a
fraud in undertaking to do so.

His is a false idealism. As the pacifist would betray the trust
of any soldiers with whom he purports to take up arms, so
this false idealist betrays the trust of the stakeholders with
whom he purports to play the game.

When you're dealing with a purely personal matter that
impacts no one but yourself, feel free to choose what extent
to play the game. But when others are counting on you, that's
foolish and disloyal.

He who embarks on a fool's errand should do so on
his own nickel.

If you're going to engage in a particular area of endeavor,
there's simply no warrant for you to believe you're too good
to play its game all out.

Yet the Entreprenati do more than play the game all
out—they also change the game. This doesn't mean breaking the rules. That would be cheating, and Entreprenati don't
cheat. It means taking the game in a new direction or to a new
level not even contemplated by its rules. This ushers in a new
game, with new rules.

The old rules weren't broken—they were eclipsed.

Now, we're not talking about exploiting a loophole, a
technicality, or some other grey area to create the illusion
that the letter of the rule is respected, while its spirit is vio-
lated. That's cheating just the same. We're not talking about
that. We're talking about the Fosbury Flop.

At the 1968 Olympics, Dick Fosbury won the gold medal and set a new record in the high jump by introducing the world to what is now known as the Fosbury Flop. Rather than leap into the air facing the bar, he did it with his back to it, so he faced up toward the sky as he flew over. He thus turned the sport 180 degrees on its head, literally. Did he break the rules? No. The rules required competitors to keep one foot on the ground at their takeoff point (which he did)—the rules didn't otherwise specify how to perform the event. Did he reinvent the game? Yes. Today, all high jumpers use the Fosbury Flop.

36

Wheel of Fortune

In determining what pursuits they'll take on in their lives and how they'll attack them, most people try to avoid, to the extent they can, those factors that are beyond their control. Problem is, there's only so much you can accomplish this way. In fact, that "so much" is not much. Let's face it, there's damn little you can control in this world.

That's where partners can come in. They can bring the funds, expertise, skills, contacts, and other resources to help control some of the factors you can't control on your own.

That's great, as far as it goes, but it doesn't go far. You're still limited in what you can accomplish because the bulk of what happens in our lives is simply beyond human control.

Now, just imagine what mind-blowing achievements would be possible if you had a partner with superhuman powers — the ability to control all the stuff that's beyond the reach of any mere mortal. If only there was such a titan ... if only you could join forces with him.

Well there is, and you can.

His name is Chance. And you can partner with him anytime you like — if you dare. You do this by taking risk.

*The bigger the risk you take in your pursuit, the
larger the role you give Chance in it as your partner
(whether or not you realize it).*

But Chance isn't the type of partner you bring in lightly.
If left to his own devices, he's a maniac, equally likely to use
his prodigious powers for or against you. Neither vindictive
nor goodhearted, he acts randomly, with no rhyme or reason
to his ways. Having this type of partner, especially one so
muscular, is a recipe for disaster.

Yet there is someone, a certain female, who can hold some
sway over him. In fact, depending on how persuasive she
chooses to be in any particular situation, she can bend his will
quite a bit. That someone is Lady Luck.

If Luck puts in a good word for you, Chance may work his
magic in your favor. But if she puts in a bad word, Chance
will probably hose you.

So, how do you get on Luck's good side and avoid her bad
side? Well, it depends on which of the Risk Brothers brings
you to the party — Smart or Stupid.

Luck and Smart Risk are bosom buddies, but Luck doesn't
get along with Stupid Risk at all. In fact, Luck has it out for
Stupid Risk and loves to rock his world whenever she can.

So, if you roll with Smart Risk, Luck will whisper sweet
things in Chance's ear about you. The tighter you stick with
Smart Risk, the more Luck will go to bat for you with Chance.

But if you roll with Stupid Risk, Luck will whisper sour
things in Chance's ear about you. The deeper you fall into the
arms of Stupid Risk, the more Luck will lean on Chance to
do you in. It's nothing personal. It's just that any friend of
Stupid Risk is an enemy of Luck.

Problem is, Stupid Risk can be a lot of fun, while Smart Risk can be a real grind. Stupid Risk doesn't make demands on you. He just wants to go for it, without weighing the upside versus the downside or considering the particulars. Smart Risk, on the other hand, he insists that you rigorously assess the situation, painstakingly plan out all the festivities, get all your ducks in a row, and then methodically execute, while monitoring for course corrections as you proceed. Don't get me wrong. He's into fun too, just a different type—he thrills to the challenge of skillfully carving out a well-earned victory in a jungle of uncertainty.

Do you have the ambition and fortitude to partner with Chance? If so, do you have the foresight and discipline to form this partnership through Smart Risk, or will you succumb to the siren song of Stupid Risk?

37

Present & Accounted For

~⌒~

Descartes doubted everything, even his very existence.

A philosopher who lived in France 400 years ago (1596-1650), René Descartes is often viewed as the father of modern philosophy. Like many philosophers before and after, he spent decades of his life contemplating man's existence.

Descartes began by doubting his perceptions, because our senses often deceive us. He then doubted a physical world exists, because it's based on our perceptions, which are in doubt. He finally concluded everything must therefore be in doubt, but one thing must be free of it — that we exist. To doubt, we must exist. *Cogito, ergo sum*, as he put it, Latin for "I think, therefore I am." To doubt is to think, and that which thinks must exist.

Hmm ... well, agree or disagree with Descartes' reasoning, his work demonstrates two cardinal things — man has long struggled with the question of his existence, and man strives mightily to believe he does in fact exist. We don't want to believe God will at some point awaken from his divine slumber and we'll disappear along with his nightly dream of which we were merely a part.

Yet the Entreprenati don't believe man exists because he thinks, but rather, because he affects.

Moveō, ergo sum—I affect, therefore I am.

In fact, the Entreprenati believe "a man *is* his effect"—that your existence lies in your effect. Your effect on others.

Yet we use the word "lies" in both its meanings. People can't always tell what, if any, effect they have on others. And they often lie to themselves, convincing themselves they've had an effect, when in fact they haven't. Knowing this, people seek validation of their effect. This, the Entreprenati believe, is driven by man's desire to validate his very existence.

That's a powerful desire. Some might say the most powerful. This is why people so desperately crave acknowledgement. It gives their life meaning. It tells them they're more than a figment of the cosmic imagination. That they matter.

Which brings us to appreciation and gratitude. The Entreprenati believe we owe it to our fellow humans to recognize when they have an effect on us and to express this recognition to them.

We have no right to deny others their existence.

When we discharge our duty to validate one another's existence, this builds a world of healthy energy around us. This, in turn, attracts people (the right kinds of people) and other wonderful things. In helping others, we also help ourselves.

Now, certain aspects of your good fortune aren't directly attributable to the effects of other people. These blessings, such as being born of able mind and body, are attributable to the hand of cards you were dealt. Some believe God is the dealer. For others, it's the Universe or some other Being or

Force. Here, again, whatever you believe in, you have a duty to appreciate and express your gratitude, even if only to the Great Unknown. This validates Its existence, as well as your own.

Grain of Sand

"Songs of life amid souls of the dead," I said to Charisse, as we enjoyed the last of our night out at one of her favorite jazz clubs — *Le Caveau des Oubliettes*, cellar of the forgotten. On the way over, she'd told me it was originally a dungeon where prisoners were tortured and killed in the twelfth century. Once at the building, we descended a small, winding staircase, ducked under an archway, and entered the dank underground chamber. Iron shackles still hung on the stone walls that bore inscriptions of the condemned who perished there.

Thinking about those whose lives ended before they were done living made me glad to be among the recently undeparted. While I couldn't put a precise date on my awakening, I knew it had arrived. On second thought, I knew I'd ushered it in.

"That really was wonderful," I said, as we left the club and began walking along *Rue Galande*.

"Yes, I adore the *boef*, it is so raw, and so different every time," she said, still shimmying to the beat in her red, form-fitting sweater dress.

"You mean the open jam session, right?

"Of course."

"Why is it called a *boef*? Isn't that the word for beef?"

"Has anyone ever told you that you ask a lot of questions?"

I grabbed Charisse, lifted her off her feet, and spun her around, as we laughed and kissed. Savoring all the pleasures of the moment, I couldn't help but marvel at my good fortune. There were so many blessings to be thankful for in my new life, and she was definitely one of them, a big one.

"We should go to an improvisational comedy show next Saturday," Charisse said, as our bodies pressed together, grinding in a slow, rhythmic swaying. "I know the best one in the city."

"I'd love to, but I'll be in Lyon with Glith then."

"Really?" she asked, lighting up like a mischievous child. "How do I know this Glith fellow actually exists? You never tell me anything about him or what you two do together. How do I know you are not seeing another woman down there?"

"Oh, he exists all right."

"So tell me about him."

Hmm, how could I even begin to describe Glith? Someone who accepts who I am, while making me wonder who that really is. Who makes me want to be that person, the true me.

"He's my grain of sand," I finally said. Oh god, I thought as soon as I uttered those words, now I'm talking like him.

"What does *that* mean?"

"I'm not really sure, but I must've been thinking of oysters ... you know, how a grain of sand could be the opportunity to create their life's masterpiece, but only if they see it this way ... and if they choose to act on it."

"Glith sounds very special. Why have you been so se-
cretive about him and what you two are up to?"

"It's complicated ... all I can say is I promised not to tell
anyone and I must honor my promise. Will you trust me
on this?"

"Yes, I will trust you," she said, tilting her head forward
so our noses touched. Then she whispered in my ear—
"*Jusqu'à la Lune ... et retour.*"

38

Imagine That

~

Every advancement that has ever occurred, from the dawn of mankind till today, began at precisely the same point. Whether in medicine, psychology, law, mathematics, government, space travel, business, or anything else, every leap forward in the human condition sprang forth from this common origin.

> *It began, as it always does, at the magical moment*
> *when someone asked— "What if?"*

This is when curiosity moves beyond our world in search of a new one.

The ability to foster this metamorphosis of curiosity from its discovery phase into its creation phase is a hallmark of the Entreprenati.

But before you can ever hope to give birth to the "what if" butterfly, you must first construct its caterpillar forbearer from the building materials of the what, how, and why.

Something's happening. People are being crippled. Buildings are bursting into flames. You're losing your grip.

Curious minds ask—what's happening? Turns out, the paralysis is caused by a virus. The buildings are being set ablaze by lightening. Your mental instability is the result of a new boss who's so toxic he's driving you to drink. Some end their inquiry there. They see only the need for wheelchairs, fire departments, and Alcoholics Anonymous.

More curious minds ask—how is this happening? They discover that the virus enters through the mouth, multiplies in the intestine, then courses through the bloodstream, and invades the central nervous system, destroying the neurons that operate the body's muscles. The electricity discharges from the clouds down onto the buildings, then travels to the ground, igniting the building as it passes through. Your new boss is generally nice, but whenever you or anyone else shares an idea with him, he mercilessly blasts into it.

Minds that are still more curious ask the deepest discovery question of all—why is this happening? Why doesn't the body fight off the virus? Turns out, the virus acts too quickly for the body to establish a defense. Why does lighting prefer to travel to the ground through buildings, rather than directly? Turns out, it's easier for electricity to travel through solid objects than through air, so it uses this path of least resistance. Why does your boss blast into people whenever they present an idea? At first, you think he's just a sadist, but then you remember he once mentioned he learned the business under a boss who "vigorously challenged" all his ideas.

With the answers to those questions—what, how, and why—you understand the situation. Many stop there, their curiosity sated.

Yet some transcend the chasm from discovery to creation. After getting answers to the what, how, and why discovery questions, they ask the magical question of creation—What if?

What if we inject people with a weakened form of the virus; would this cause their bodies to establish a defense before they got infected? What if we place a metal rod high on each building, with a wire running down to the ground; would lightening strike the rod and travel down the wire, rather than through the building? What if I sit down with my boss and explain that his technique of "vigorous challenge" isn't working for me, and is actually ruining my life; would this trigger a change in his behavior?

> *The Entreprenati question everything. They question problems, unwilling to accept their right to exist. They question assumptions, unwilling to accept their truth at face value. They question rules, unwilling to accept their constraints. They question the current order, unwilling to accept its inevitability.*

They question the what, how, and why of everything. Then, once they understand today, they unleash the "what if" — in the quest for a better tomorrow.

The magic of "what if" knows no bounds. It operates across every realm — in science, business, government, your family life, the arts, you name it.

What if you create a what if journal to track the what ifs you're posing to yourself and to the world? What if you challenge yourself to ask what ifs every day, and hold yourself accountable for follow-through on them? What if you also challenge yourself to identify the problems, assumptions, rules, and elements of the current order you're now failing to subject to the rigors of the what, how, and why, and the magic of the what if? What if you do none of this?

39

Out of the Box and into the Fire

What do you do with a guy like Arsenio?

When Arsenio worked at Pretty Good But Not So Great Company, he found himself taking on less of the traditional types of work and devoting substantial effort toward redesigning the company's business model. He didn't consciously decide to split his time this way, it just happened. That's the kind of guy he is. While others focused on always being "busy" with the day to day and avoiding anything that could be perceived as "downtime," Arsenio went out on a limb seeking to find ways the company might do things differently.

This caused dissension within the ranks. They felt that much of Arsenio's time was wasted and they resented that he "had the luxury to contemplate how many angels could dance on the head of a pin." Arsenio's boss tolerated this atmosphere. This pressured Arsenio to get back in line. It also pressured him to start innovating right away and to avoid any experimentation that might be perceived as failure. Does this sound like your company?

This kind of atmosphere kills innovation.

Innovation requires commitment of time and a willingness to experiment in ways that fail more often than they succeed.

So Arsenio found a job at another company, where his boss actively supported him as an innovator. His new boss realized his people were largely homogeneous in their adherence to common beliefs and behaviors. Arsenio had a clear mandate to devote substantial time toward dreaming up new ideas, rather than just busying himself with the work of the day. He was properly positioned for this, given the appropriate authority, resources, and incentive, and it was openly acknowledged that behind every innovation is a scrap heap of failed experiments. This empowered and motivated Arsenio to seek to change the rules of the game — and he did.

If you're an executive, which sort of organization should you be running? If you're like Arsenio (or aspire to be like him), which sort of organization should you be working at? If you're one of the drones who would prefer to crush Arsenio's creative spirits, then by all means carry on — someone's got to be part of the undifferentiated mass of human flesh that mindlessly churns out the daily grind, and that, my friend, would be you.

It takes all types to run a business. If everyone tried to change things, the company would never get its work done. You need the worker bees for that. But if no one changes things, then at some point there won't be any work for the bees to do — the market will pass you by. Customers will move on to the new products and services offered by your competitors. Or to less expensive ones made possible by advances in business efficiencies forged by your competitors.

Problem is, most people, if left to their own devices, won't seek innovation. They lack confidence in their ability to do so. They're unwilling to incur resentment. They fear that failed experiments might damage their careers. They doubt their companies will be open to new ideas, much less value them. They feel that incremental results will keep them employed, whereas the company may lose patience with the longer-term commitment required to fuel innovation. They fear for their job security if they aren't perceived as performing standard functions.

Do you have any innovators in your organization? Do you seek them out? Do you cultivate them? Do you recruit them? Have you properly positioned, empowered, and incented them? Have you created an atmosphere in which intelligent risk-taking and efficient-failure are embraced as essential components of an active experimental culture? Have you worked to address the resentment others naturally harbor toward innovators?

If you're an innovator (or aspire to be one), are you working in your own business or in an organization that supports innovation—or is it that you just groove to the sound of your head knocking against a wall?

40

Chain Reaction

～

Ever meet a quark? Me neither. But this doesn't mean we're not social people. After all, those quarks don't get out much. They stay inside their atom homes, with their proton nucleus family and electron friends. Sight unseen, though, they rule the world. In fact, they are the world.

It's sometimes said these days that small is the new big. Truth be told, however, it always has been.

People are forever hoping to "hit it big" — get the big job, land the big client, invent the next big thing. They ask themselves — what big actions are required to achieve these big things? Want to know the answer? Here it is: None.

> *The key to achieving big things lies in doing little things.*

Sound easy? It's actually so difficult that few ever get it right.

Here's the problem — when you begin doing the little things, you don't see much in the way of results. And this sorry state of affairs continues for quite a while. So, while you're slaving away doing the little things you need to do if you're ever going to be successful, your friends are out having fun, and it looks like they have the better idea. Neither of you is showing any tangible movement toward success, but at least they're enjoying themselves. You, not so much.

It doesn't take long for common logic to prevail. Soon, you're off with your friends, the little things are going undone, and the prospects of your success fade to black.

What's missing from this picture?

Think of a catapult. You turn the winch, little by little, and a spring-loaded mechanism continuously builds up potential energy. As you turn and turn and turn the winch, nothing much happens. The potential energy just builds and builds and builds. You can't see it, but it's there. Yet it remains merely potential energy at that point. If you give up before the mechanism is ready to launch, you wind up with nothing. But if you keep going until it's set, then you can climb aboard and release the ratchet, converting the potential energy into a torrent of power that'll propel you skyward.

But to see this from where you are now requires vision. Even with that vision, however, you'll also need staying power, and lots of it. This means willingness to work long and hard, to sacrifice immediate gratification, to endure peer pressure, to believe in yourself. You can do all that, right?

41

Lunar Navigation

Pity the salesman striving to sell cars, the lawyer striving to win cases, the dancer striving for flawless moves.

Whatever something may seem to be about, it's not.
It's always about something else.

The salesman is selling not cars, but dreams — the dream of adventure to the young couple striking out on their own, the dream of freedom to the old man too frail to bear the rigors of public transportation, the dream of raising a family to the breadwinner who must drive to work.

The lawyer provides protection to his vulnerable clients who are under siege in a fearsome system they can scarcely comprehend, much less control. Of course this includes striving to win the case, but it means much more. The case may last for years — the client seeks peace of mind for himself and his family throughout that embattled time. What the client is really looking for is refuge from the storm.

The dancer struts her stuff not so she may be perceived as flawless, but as captivating, evocative, poignant, stirring. The audience seeks release from the maddening blandness of the day to day, to escape into a rhythmic fascination of mind and body.

To the casual observer, the human world consists of what people say and do. As you go through your day, that's what's all around you—people saying and doing things. But those words and acts are merely manifestations of underlying needs and desires. Those needs and desires are what our world is really about.

When someone walks into a Starbucks for a coffee, for instance, that's not what it's really about. Starbucks provides a warm inviting respite from the chaos that is otherwise your life, conveniently located for immediate gratification, where you can buy something at a price obscene enough to validate your fine taste, worth, and entitlement, delivered by hip baristas, as jazzy music, pleasant aromas, and soft lighting soothe your senses, making you feel pampered and part of the "in crowd." Even after you leave the store, there's the exalted status of being seen with the Starbucks cup—you're a member of an honored club. That's what Starbucks is really about.

The same applies to all aspects of life. Your wife rips into you for not taking out the garbage. It's a safe bet her anger isn't really about the garbage. She's feeling unloved ... or she's distressed over a work-related situation ... or she's worried sick about the family's finances ... or something else. You need to take a peek under the hood—find out what it's really about. Ditto for understanding your friends, colleagues, customers, vendors, competitors, and others, including yourself.

When you observe the tides of the ocean and realize you're actually observing the phases of the moon, you become more mindful of a truer reality.

42

The Usual Suspects

~

When Steffen joined Lacuna Corporation as the new head of its Tatterdemalion Division, he quickly discovered that the division operated poorly. The company was profitable and well run overall, but not his division.

So he designed a change agenda called "Project Excellence." It involved appointing each employee to one of three "consultant teams" and to one of three "client teams." Through a series of exercises Steffen created, each consultant team would analyze the work of each client team. The exercises were to involve daily interactions, weekly meetings, and various presentations. The idea was to foster group discovery, as each employee would act as a consultant regarding some types of work and as a client regarding other types. The employees were to collectively analyze the division's processes and devise ways to improve them.

But the project didn't go as planned. Rather than welcome it, the employees resisted it heart and soul. The teamwork was nonexistent to dysfunctional and Steffen never did get it on track. Project Excellence was a complete bust. After a few months, he scrapped it entirely.

So, what did Steffen learn from this inglorious misadventure? Nothing and everything. Nothing he didn't already know, but everything needed to make this knowledge truly meaningful to him. After all—

We meet the usual suspects of life's basic causes and effects early on, only to spend the rest of our days discovering who these folks really are.

How did Steffen get better acquainted with a few of the usual suspects here? Let us count (some of) the ways ...

For starters, and most fundamentally, Steffen ran into Miss Framing. She's the nasty gremlin who sets you chasing after the wrong problem from the get-go. Steffen thought he could fix the performance issues by reengineering the inefficient processes, but he should have recognized they were but a symptom of a deeper problem—the culture. When a group has been stuck in a low performance mode for a long time, it's a pretty safe bet the culture is moribund. Without the foundation of a strong and productive culture, excellent processes are an impossibility. Steffen already knew Miss Framing, or so he thought—now he has the opportunity to really know her (if his mind is open to such learning).

Then there was Mandate Gap. The employees didn't see the need for change. The company did fine overall and so the employees were feeling no pain. Absent pain, people don't ordinarily see any mandate for change. This is a mistake, but that's the way it is with most rank and file, especially those mired in a weak culture. Endeavoring to design an improvement requires a particular type of foresight and discipline when things are basically going well and the change is called for in the company's longer-term interests. Run of the mill workers rarely possess such qualities. To address this gap,

Steffen should have made clear the pressure for change. The employees needed to feel the heat. Steffen already knew all this too, or so he thought—now he has the opportunity to really know it (if his mind is open to such learning).

Also at the party was Mandate Gap's cousin, Desiré Gap. The employees didn't share Steffen's desire for change. While strong cultures often hail improvements, especially when they're needed but even when they're not, weak cultures live in dread of any change, positive or otherwise. Steffen should have done a better job emphasizing the benefits participants would derive from the change (smoother work flow, personal and professional growth, career enhancement, and future potential pay increases and/or bonuses). Steffen also should have tapped a few people to serve as evangelists who would generate positive buzz around the project, energizing everyone toward desiring the change. Steffen already knew all this too, or so he thought—now he has the opportunity to really know it (if his mind is open to such learning).

Not to be left out was Credibility Deficit. In the eyes of the employees, Steffen lacked credibility as a change agent. Change agents are often viewed with suspicion concerning their motives and/or ability to effect the change. As a new person with an aggressive style and little established rapport, trust, or allegiance, Steffen was subject to such suspicion. He should have spent some time cultivating relationships before storming into such an ambitious project like a bull in a china shop. This would have allowed others to appreciate his motives and abilities, and allowed him to gain a better read on the people and the situation. He also should have bolstered his credibility by making it clear he was backed by strong executive sponsorship (if indeed he was, which could have been another problem operating against the project if he wasn't). Steffen already knew all this too, or so he thought—now he has the opportunity to really know it (if his mind is open to such learning).

Present as well was Complexity Demon. Implementing a project is never easy, but it gets exponentially harder when we try something elaborate. Too many moving parts that can go awry. Steffen already knew all this too, or so he thought—now he has the opportunity to really know it (if his mind is open to such learning).

Also lurking about was the gaping Objectivity Hole. The folks who create or perpetuate a problem are seldom the right ones to correct it. While the insiders' input is valuable, yet an outside perspective is vital to designing the best solution in most cases. Steffen already knew all this too, or so he thought—now he has the opportunity to really know it (if his mind is open to such learning).

And further muddying the waters was the ever-unsightly Vision In Absentia. The employees weren't told how any possible solution might fit into any larger vision. Of course the final implementation couldn't be known until the solution was conceived, yet people still need to be given some idea of how the leader intends to carry out the change and how that change fits into the leader's larger vision. Steffen already knew all this too, or so he thought—now he has the opportunity to really know it (if his mind is open to such learning).

Most importantly, there was an overall failure of leadership. Utilizing a "leadership by committee" methodology meant the blind leading the blind here. The employees were weak performers; they needed a leader. It's important to make everyone feel involved, but Steffen should have empowered a single change agent to lead the way—either himself or a potent leader within his group (if there was any), or he should have brought in an outsider for this role. In this and many other ways, Steffen didn't do what was necessary to overcome the various obstacles that existed. He also failed to demonstrate that he had the authority to enforce any negative consequences for his employees' intransigence. Steffen already knew all this too, or so he thought—now he has the opportunity to really know it (if his mind is open to such learning).

Even if one does everything right, driving change through an organization is never easy. When you do a few things wrong, the effort is often doomed. Do a lot wrong and failure is pretty much inevitable. This yields only the opportunity for lessons to be learned—an opportunity for you to reap to great benefit or squander to great shame.

By the way, saying Steffen already knew about the problems with his approach before his misadventure began doesn't mean to diminish the tremendous (potential) value of the learning opportunity this debacle represents in his development.

> *Words have yet to be invented to adequately describe the gulf between an understanding derived from study or observation versus an understanding born of personal failure.*

While we should never seek failure nor welcome it, when it does nevertheless darken our doorstep, we should embrace the bounty of (potential) learning it showers upon us. The learning that can flow from personal failure holds the promise of a richness in meaning no other source of wisdom can ever hope to match.

PART VI

GET IT TOGETHER

September Meeting

Over a month had passed since I last met with Glith and nearly two weeks since we last spoke. Most disturbingly, he hadn't returned my calls. That was unusual, so I decided to phone his doorman to see what I could learn. He said Glith was laid up in bed. That news rattled me. I decided to go to him right away.

On the train, I started thinking about how our relationship had so completely changed over the last year. Before I'd come to France, Glith was like the uncle who appears out of nowhere when needed. More of a shining figure than a real person. But now he'd become very real. And more than family. He'd become a true friend. A hard place to get to in my world. Yet lately, the door to who I am had opened — not only for people on the outside, but for me too.

After a two-hour ride that seemed to take forever, I finally reached Lyon and rushed over to Glith's building on that chilly September night.

When I arrived, the doorman buzzed Glith's apartment, but got no answer. I guess my mind must've assumed the worst — a knot violently welled up in my stomach and I nearly keeled over. But just then the phone rang; it was Glith. I made my way over to the elevator, my stomach still wrenched. I tried to stretch it out on the ride up.

As the elevator opened, I saw Glith in his doorway. Seeing he was okay, I relaxed. "Where else would you live but the top floor?" I asked, composing myself.

"There's always the roof," he replied. "Come in Jesse. Welcome to my humble abode." He bowed slightly and gestured me in.

There was nothing humble about the place. Although the outside of the building and the lobby were plain, his apartment was ultramodern and super high-end. I'd never been there before, but I guess it shouldn't have surprised me.

"You clean up nicely when you want to," he quipped. "And that's a new suit if I'm not mistaken."

"You're not mistaken and I'll take that as a compliment. I wish I could say the same about you. But, then again, I thought I'd find you on your deathbed, gasping your last breath, quill in hand, penning your book till the end."

"I wouldn't be *that* melodramatic ... maybe a Waterman pen, but not a quill. Come, I have coffee and croissants in the kitchen."

We walked into the kitchen, which was the size of my entire apartment, and I sat at the table. Glith brought me a cup and sat next to me, on the same side of the table.

"I'm glad to see you're up and about," I said, as I poured myself a drink. "I was worried when I hadn't heard from you in so long."

"Well, I'm glad you didn't just wait for me to call, and decided to come."

"Was this some kind of test?"

"Test? No, not at all," he said, as he lifted a croissant and dipped it into his coffee. "But you do have good timing. I finished the next group of chapters and planned to call you soon, hoping to feel a touch better first."

"You know, my friend, you shouldn't wait to feel better before calling me. I feel better every time I hear your voice. I could only hope to have a similar effect on you."

Glith just stared at me, smiling and gently nodding his head for a while.

"So what's new in your world?" he finally said, breaking out of his stare and reaching for his cup.

"Well, you know I've been learning how to use the 3D graphics program that I bought and getting involved in the CGI community."

"Yes, and how's it going?"

"It's definitely going, I'll tell you that. Listen to this — I was talking to a guy who works in the field and he mentioned a project he was struggling with, and I suggested he come at it a different way, and guess what?"

"What?"

"We found an innovative solution — we! Him *and* me. He even told his boss, the owner of the company, that I was involved in it."

"Congratulations, your efforts are paying off. That's wonderful news."

"And get this! Now we're talking about me interning for the company while I go to school! That's a great in, and it'll really accelerate my learning."

"Wow!" said Glith, as he reached over and hugged me hard and for a long time. He'd never done that before. It made me feel proud and grateful, but also an eerie sense of goodbyes unspoken.

We spent a few more hours together. I tried to find out about Glith's medical condition, but, as usual, he wouldn't talk about it. We discussed the chapters of his book I'd read so far and, for the first time, he mentioned a few things about the next set of chapters I hadn't read yet.

—

After a very long train ride, I finally arrived back at my apartment. No question I wouldn't be getting much sleep that night. I opened the envelope and began inhabiting the next group of Glith's chapters ...

43

Frankly my Dear,
I Do Give a Damn

~

Caring enough to do things right is the hallmark of the Entreprenati. This means caring enough to think, feel, and act with passion and excellence; to be true to yourself and others; to do the painful things that should be done; and to never fail those who rely on you.

These are so much more than mere words to the Entreprenati. We're talking about a deep and abiding conviction to care, and all that goes into reaching toward this ideal with every fiber of one's being.

The most fundamental thing that goes into it is a commitment to act honorably in everything we do. To faithfully discharge this duty we each owe to one another. There's no finer gift we can give of ourselves, or to ourselves. No greater calling we can answer.

But there's a problem:

While it's human to want to do the good, yet it's also human to suffer from weaknesses and failings that limit the full expression of our will to do so.

Those weaknesses and failings cheapen us in myriad ways. Other chapters discuss many of them and their ill effects.

Here, we'll focus on what's perhaps the most insidious one of all—self-induced blindness.

When faced with a situation calling upon you to take action that would require sacrifice, hardship, or some other pain, you have a tough decision to make—answer the call, or shrink from it. A tough decision, but a fair question. What kind of person are you? The situation is calling you out. Forcing you to reveal your true self. That's what's happening. Yet most people never see it.

Your perception and perspective work for you. Like any working stiff, they don't want to show their boss what he doesn't want to see. Like any boss, you send out signals indicating what you don't want to see.

Since you don't want to believe you'd shrink from doing the painful things that should be done, you let your perception and perspective know you don't want to be shown facts and views that would call upon you to do anything painful.

Voila! Problem solved—your perception and perspective do your dirty work for you.

You're free to enjoy a life blind to inconvenient realities and to fancy yourself the kind of person who wouldn't fail to act nobly, even under trying conditions.

If you want to be a true standup person, rather than a poser, you must remain vigilantly aware of your mind's power to contort your perception and perspective, and you must actively strive to combat this—to see things as they actually are.

The Entreprenati live truthful lives, no matter how
painful this might be in some circumstances.

Stop signaling to your perception and perspective that
you want a self-serving picture of what's going on around
you. Instruct your perception and perspective to show it to
you straight. Challenge yourself each and every day—what
unwelcome truths are you hiding from yourself?

Strive to identify your weaknesses and failings that are
limiting the expression of your spirit to act with the highest
worthiness. Strive to find the means to free your spirit from
those limitations. Make it an obsession, as though your very
humanity hangs in the balance—because it does.

Stripped down to the naked essence of what it
means to be human, all that remains is your per-
sonal integrity.

Your personal integrity as expressed through your honorable action. Unexpressed integrity—honorable intention
not translated into action—withers and rots like fruit abandoned on the vine to the ravages of time.

It's necessarily a work in progress. What's important is to
care enough to pull out all the stops, to keep at it, consciously
and deliberately, and to be honest with yourself and others
about how you're doing.

After all the dust settles, you're defined by what you do.
So you should do the right thing. It's really that simple—and
that complex.

44

I'll Just Let Myself In, Thank You

~

Tammy's bummed because she was born a worker bee, rather than a queen bee. When she was developing as a larvae, she wasn't anointed worthy of being fed the royal jelly, so she didn't get to become a queen bee. This decision was made for her by others. That's the way it is in her world. Hey, I feel for her. Glad I'm no bee.

You're no bee either, but a bee you be.

Society's like a hive, with its many drone and worker bees and its relatively few kings and queens. Sure, it's possible to become a king or queen, but only if the royalty accept you into the castle. It's their call, not yours.

In contrast, remember what I said about the Entreprenati—membership can't be given, it must be taken.

The Entreprenati don't allow others to define them.

They don't allow others to decide if they can or cannot become kings or queens. Nor do they allow their circumstances to decide their fate. Not their circumstances of birth. Not the circumstances they later encounter. Not anything.

When you emerge from your paper bag, you're making a bold statement. You're declaring to yourself and to the rest of the world that, from now on, you'll be taking 100% responsibility for your success or failure.

No excuses.

That's not to say you won't be seeking support from others. But it'll be *your* responsibility to determine the type and timing of support you need, and *your* responsibility to go out and get it. You should be thankful to those who lend a hand, but the success will be yours. You may be bitter at those who let you down, but the failure will be yours.

In a traditional life, others can stop you from achieving your dreams. Bust out of your paper bag, however, and you'll be in a place where nobody else can stop you. Where only you can stop you. Unfortunately, most people aren't up to the challenge of facing themselves on the battlefield. But now you are.

45

It's Not an Option

The most valuable things on Earth are those that are the rarest. Among human qualities, the rarest of all is trustworthiness.

It's not a natural quality. The law of the jungle is to the contrary. And, as anyone will tell you, despite all of man's advances, it's still a jungle out there.

Being trustworthy has three dimensions. It means others can rest assured you'll: (1) act honestly & fairly, (2) get the job done, and (3) keep your word.

It's the rare individual who can command full trustworthiness, especially across all three of its dimensions.

Each of us possess certain abilities. Yet the value of those abilities is debased if the person isn't fully trustworthy. What good is any ability if others can't trust you to use it honestly & fairly, or if you're unreliable, or if you don't keep your word? Being untrustworthy poisons all your qualities.

Being trustworthy, on the other hand, dramatically boosts the value of your qualities. In fact, it's such a potent amplifier that none other comes close to matching its astonishing power of magnification.

Trust exists along a spectrum. At one end, you wouldn't trust someone any farther than you could throw them. At the other, you'd trust them with your life.

In today's somewhat civilized society, most people come out more to the positive end of this spectrum. But when it comes to trustworthiness, it's not a linear thing. You see, even if someone's 80% trustworthy, this still means they're essentially untrustworthy. Only when you get damn near 100% do you become truly trustworthy. Few ever achieve this.

The tragedy and mystery of it all is that each of us holds the power to become magnificent simply by being trustworthy.

Unfortunately, even if you were convinced of its paramount eminence, you couldn't simply choose to become trustworthy. It can't be the result of a choice. It can only be the result of a nonchoice.

You can be trustworthy only if being untrustworthy isn't an option for you.

It must be an article of faith, not a calculation. In any given situation, a calculation is always susceptible to a recalculation. That's why it can never serve as the foundation of trust.

Though the atheist may be convinced of the benefits of believing in God, he can't simply turn on this belief in the hope of achieving these benefits. The same is true of trustworthiness.

But how does one gain such faith? How do you become the kind of person who simply doesn't entertain any notion of acting dishonestly or unfairly, or of not finishing what you start, or of not keeping your word? The answer is that you can't— not directly. Fortunately, though, nature abhors a vacuum.

> *If you can achieve significant overall personal growth, your trustworthiness will grow itself into alignment with the bigger you.*

Consider your physical body as an analogy. There are some parts you can't directly target for improvement, yet if you grow your overall level of health, those untargetable parts will grow healthier as well.

Trustworthiness isn't the only quality that's an outgrowth of personal growth. There are many such qualities. This is yet another reason why working to improve yourself yields fruit that multiply geometrically more abundant as you make your progress. At some point, if you keep at it, you can experience an explosion of growth—as all the elements of being a great being start to kick in and gel. It's as if the different facets of you are lifting up one another as they themselves are being lifted, drawing up the whole of you to a higher plane of unity.

46

I Was Found, But Now I'm Lost

Herman Hesse's novel, *Siddhartha*, is the story of a young man who embarks on a journey in search for his fulfillment. Along the way, he comes across a kind stranger who asks what he needs, and Siddhartha says he doesn't need anything. The stranger then inquires about Siddhartha's possessions, and Siddhartha says he has none.

> *Wandering alone in the world, with nothing but his loincloth, yet in need of nothing. In need of nothing, yet tirelessly seeking his fulfillment.*

Like Siddhartha, you can and should demand no less than everything you yearn from life, but at the same time recognize that you don't actually need anything more than you already have.

> *You should be at once both a merry sojourner and a restless seeker.*

Forever in active search of the larger purpose life holds for you, a purpose that will empower you to make the most of your time here, to help others, and to do the most good, yet also blessed with an endless appreciation for all that you have and a need for nothing more ... as you go about in a life that appears to you as a series of adventures — adventures that have their low points, and adventures that could always get better, but glorious adventures nonetheless.

Let this dichotomy of spirit (merry sojourner/restless seeker) shape all aspects of your being. Let it drive you to persist in a fierce development mode — building yourself up through continuous self-discovery and personal growth, so you can be a totally different, more powerful presence each year than the year before.

You should find yourself to be a miraculous being for each current model year, yet totally unacceptable and in need of reengineering for the next.

> *Love yourself enough to appreciate who you are, yet love yourself even more by appreciating who you could be.*

Fueled by the miracle of unremitting self-love, you may hope to create your truest destiny, and to become worthy of its challenges.

Never cease growing toward your fulfillment. Unlike most people, who live in fear and dread of change, you should embrace change as a valued lifelong companion. Only with this ally by your side can you ever become what you could be.

While the young are told they may have to settle for less when they grow up, you should believe — whatever your age — that you have a long time to go before that'll ever happen to you. Remain a child of the universe. There are no Entreprenati among the grownups.

47

All Hands on Deck

~

People truly are their own worst enemies, and the most damaging of their self-inflicted wounds come from deceiving themselves, running from themselves, and hiding from themselves.

We humans exist in multiple dimensions of self — the Thinking Self, Feeling Self, Remembering Self, Spiritual Self, Physical Self, Sensing Self, Subconscious Self, and other selves, known and unknown. These selves are constantly sabotaging one another through deception, concealment, and abandonment. It's a jungle in there.

To be Entreprenati is to be dedicated to the ceaseless drawing together of these selves into a greater harmony.

The starting point is to see all these selves running amuck inside you. Shine a bright light within. Let it illuminate all the dark recesses, the hiding spots, the chambers of deception.

Call out your selves. Call them out into the open. Into the light. Make them show themselves — to you, and to one another.

Next, once you're eyeball to eyeball with all your selves, it's time to lead them. Make them stop working at cross purposes. Make them pull together as a cohesive team—Team You.

Your selves are your internal personal organization. You need to be the leader of this organization. Otherwise, your internal personal organization will be in disarray.

As with any organization, the members will each have their own individual strengths and weaknesses, as well as differences of opinion, style, and approach to things. That's fine, as long as they share a common mission under strong leadership. No one else but you can provide this leadership.

If you want to embark on your path to the Entreprenati, you'll need to be a leader. First and foremost, you'll need to be a self-leader.

> *Your Leading Self must step up and take its rightful place as the head of your internal personal organization—to rally, inspire, and manage your selves, and to hold them accountable.*

Your Leading Self must create and maintain an environment in which your various selves can flourish, individually and collectively as a whole—a whole you.

The poet T.S. Eliot once wrote, "We shall not cease from exploration, and the end of all our exploring will be to arrive where we started and know the place for the first time." The place where we all start is with ourselves. At birth, we are one with ourselves, but unable to know ourselves. Our selves then take on lives of their own, and we become many. We become internally divided.

The path to the Entreprenati is paved with self-ex-
ploration and the quest to regain the harmony that
graced us at birth—and to know it for the first time.

To become Entreprenati is to be born yet again, not just once
again, but over and over again.

The Letter

Nineteen days after giving me the last part of his book, Glith was gone.

The funeral hall was packed with mourners. Glith seemed like such a private guy; I had no idea he knew so many people.

A man appeared out of the crowd and handed me a small envelope. "Mr. Glithman wanted you to have this," he said. Then he also gave me his card and said I could contact him if I chose to do so. I went off to a quiet area, sat down, opened the envelope, and found a letter inside ...

Dear Jesse,

Just a brief note to apologize for telling you a small fib. I told you I wrote my manuscript because I planned to publish it, but that wasn't the real reason. I wrote it for you.

I hope you'll forgive me for being less than fully candid. I meant well. After your mother died, you seemed lost. So I made arrangements through my contacts to have your company offer you a two-year

*post in Paris. I thought the change might do you good
and the international exposure might expand your
horizons. I hoped you would choose to accept the
post. I also hoped you would choose to look me up and
spend some time with me here if you did. I was glad
to see you made those choices.*

*Once I got to know you better, I could see your
potential. I planned to mentor you in the coming
years, but then received the bad news about my health
and realized I couldn't be around for you much longer.
So I decided to write down some of our guiding
principles in ways I believed could be meaningful to
you, both then and as a reference after I moved on.*

Wishing you your best in your life's adventure,

Joe

*P.S. Remember, whoever you are, whatever you yearn
to do, if you don't do it, there's always just one reason.*

—

I folded the letter and leaned back in my chair. I looked
at the card the man had given me. It had a symbol on it
and nothing else. I smiled. Even after "moving on" as Glith
put it, he's still sending me in search of answers. Who was
that man who gave me the card? How will I contact him?
What did Glith mean by that "one reason" in the riddle at
the end of his letter?

Then I remembered something Glith said in the very first part of his book. That our ultimate fulfillment exists in seeking full expression of our own individual spirit as unique human beings, yet most people live inside a paper bag that blocks us from even seeing this possibility, much less seizing it.

It was at that moment when I realized what it means to be Entreprenati — it means to emerge from my paper bag and begin the journey to my true self. To confront my own thoughts, my own feelings, and my own behaviors that are keeping me from me.

That's what Glith meant when he said that the Entreprenati believe in their ability to forge their own path through the thicket of human experience to bring themselves to their own success. Not to "arrive" at success, as if carried there in a chariot driven by others, but to bring yourself there, under your own power, in your own way, in your own time. Not success as others define it, but your own success, as you yourself define it. That is my challenge.

Will I succeed? Will I summon the strength, the self-knowledge, the self-love? Time will tell. But I know this much. I *will* answer the call. From this day forward, I will strive to think for myself, find my own truths, perceive and make my own choices, take full responsibility for my own decisions and my own actions, all while thrilling to the chase of my own future, come what may. I will embark on my own path to the Entreprenati.

How about you? Will I see you out there?

Author's Note

Shortly after being released from prison, while I was homeless and living out of garbage cans, I was nearly killed in a freak street accident, wound up hospitalized in a coma, and then, eight months later, after the doctors had written me off, I miraculously awoke from that vegetative state and suddenly saw everything in a new light.

Nah, I'm not that guy. My worldview wasn't shocked into me by some monumental event. I wasn't that lucky. Sure, I grew up poor and endured my fair share of hard knocks, but so what. That wasn't it either. Of course all this stuff played a role. An important one. Yet ultimately, my worldview is the result of a choice. Pure and simple.

And you can make this choice too.

I'm not saying you should. It's not for everyone. But I am saying you should see the choice. My hope is that this book will help you see it. And help you succeed in your brave new world if you do choose to bust out of your personal paper bag.

Unfortunately, as Glith observed, most people will squander the opportunity and remain blind to the choice. Of those who do bring the choice into their view, most will fail the challenge it poses. Which camp will you fall into? Will you let this chance slip away or will you seize it? Will you rise to the occasion or will you shrink from it?

I hope you actually make the choice. Whether you decide to venture beyond or to remain securely ensconced within, at least you'll have faced up to the choice. I hope you'll respect yourself enough to do that. There's no shame in deciding to stay in a safe place. But ducking the decision, that's another story altogether. It's the cheap way out. And, as with most things in life, what's cheap is actually what costs you most dearly. In this case, it costs a chunk of your very humanity. A big chunk. Free will is our most precious gift. Letting it waste away is a shame.

So, embrace your humanity, exercise your free will, and make the choice. And if you do decide to join me and others in our infinite foolishness, let's all share in the excitement of our adventure together. You know where to find us.